111 Prompts for ChatGPT, Microsoft Copilot and Other Chatbots for Business Leadership

111 Prompts for ChatGPT, Microsoft Copilot and Other Chatbots for Business Leadership

Effectively Navigate Business Challenges with Artificial Intelligence for Superior Leadership and Strategic Impact

Mindscape Artwork Publishing
Mauricio Vasquez

Toronto, Canada

Authors:
Mauricio Vasquez

First Printing: November 2023

ISBN-978-1-990709-90-6 (Paperback)

ISBN-978-1-998402-17-5 (Hardcover)

DEDICATION

To all those dedicated to professional growth and effective leadership: May this book serve as your comprehensive manual, providing you with the strategies and perspectives needed to thrive in today's competitive workplace.

INTRODUCTION

Welcome to an indispensable resource that synergizes the foundational principles of mentoring, coaching, and leadership with the transformative capabilities of Generative Artificial Intelligence (AI). Crafted by Mauricio Vasquez, an expert in professional advancement and AI-empowered strategies, this book is aimed at professionals from all walks of life who have a common aim—to create a lasting impact in their circles of influence.

In the constantly evolving professional world, where adaptability, ingenuity, and substantive influence are the cornerstones of success, this book stands as your comprehensive roadmap. Enriched by the precision and adaptability of Generative AI, we go the extra mile to offer you not just tried-and-true strategies but also customized solutions that are data-backed and results-oriented.

The use of Generative AI in this book isn't ornamental; it's instrumental. This book elucidates how this revolutionary technology can be harnessed to fine-tune mentorship, amplify coaching techniques, and enliven leadership approaches.

The core objective is clear—to elevate your skill sets and tactical acumen, irrespective of your career stage or professional landscape. Whether you're an industry novice, a mid-career professional, or a seasoned leader, this handbook marries practical know-how with avant-garde advice to offer a unique blend of actionable insights.

This book does more than provide you with a set of tools; it invites you to participate in a seismic shift in professional interactions and leadership paradigms. Gear up for comprehensive explorations into the art of meaningful conversations, the precision of AI-crafted prompts, and the balance of impactful leadership.

As we set forth on this transformative journey, the aim is clear: to catapult you toward unprecedented levels of professional mastery and personal fulfillment. Welcome to the vanguard of professional development.

ABOUT THE AUTHOR

Mauricio Vasquez is a multifaceted professional with over 20 years of experience in risk management and insurance, specializing in sectors like mining, power, and renewable energy. He holds an Industrial Engineering degree, a Master's in Business Administration, and a Master's in Marketing and Commercial Management, along with certifications in Enterprise Risk Management and Artificial Intelligence.

Mauricio is also a certified Adler Trained Coach and a self-published author, focusing on personal growth and professional development. His expertise in Artificial Intelligence and Large Language Models Prompt engineering adds a unique layer to his professional background. Fluent in both English and Spanish, Mauricio has worked across Canada, the U.S., Latin America, and the Caribbean. In addition to his corporate roles, he is a Professional and Life Coach, committed to helping immigrants transition successfully to new lives in Canada. His approach is deeply rooted in building long-term relationships and providing tailored, impactful solutions to clients.

If you want to connect with Mauricio, go to this link https://www.linkedin.com/in/mauriciovasquez or scan this QR code:

WHAT IS GENERATIVE ARTIFICIAL INTELLIGENCE (AI)?

In the advanced landscape of Artificial Intelligence (AI), Generative AI emerges not merely as an incremental milestone but as a transformative narrative that reconfigures the potential of what AI can achieve. This is not a slight enhancement in the realm of data analytics. Rather, it's artificial intelligence capable of generating text, images, or other media, using generative models.

Traditional AI systems are proficient at analyzing and interpreting existing data sets. In contrast, Generative AI elevates this capability by producing entirely original content that is imbued with value. This spans a range of applications, from the composition of persuasive emails to the formulation of comprehensive strategic initiatives and the improvement of coaching dialogues. In essence, Generative AI enhances human capabilities and fundamentally alters the pathways for innovative solutions.

Built on complex neural network architectures, Generative AI goes beyond mere mimicry to acquire and extend intricate patterns of human behavior. The impact of this technology is broad and significant, affecting diverse industries such as marketing, executive leadership, and even individual personal development. It is important to note that this is not a theoretical construct confined to research labs; it is a practical innovation with immediate and expansive real-world applications.

As the industry shifts its focus to upcoming developments in Natural Language Processing (NLP) and Chatbots, it is imperative to acknowledge that Generative AI constitutes the foundational architecture for these advanced conversational interfaces. Specifically, in areas such as coaching, mentoring, and leadership development, Generative AI enriches these platforms by facilitating not just relevant, but also deeply contextual and emotionally nuanced dialogues. The outcome is an enhanced coaching model that is underpinned by both data-driven and human-like insights. Neglecting the capabilities of Generative AI would be to bypass a plethora of opportunities for innovation and increased effectiveness that this technology generously affords.

WHAT ARE NATURAL LANGUAGE PROCESSING CHATBOTS?

An Artificial Intelligence (AI) Chatbot is a program within a website or app that uses machine learning (ML) and natural language processing (NLP) to interpret inputs and understand the intent behind a request or "prompt" (more on this later in the book). Chatbots can be rule-based with simple use cases or more advanced and able to handle multiple conversations.

The rise of language models like GPT has revolutionized the landscape of conversational AI. These Chatbots now boast advanced capabilities that can mimic not just a human conversation style but also a (super) human mind. They can find information online and produce unique content and insights.

The most important thing to know about an AI Chatbot is that it combines ML and NLP to understand what people need and bring the best answers. Some AI Chatbots are better for personal use, like conducting research, and others are best for business use, like featuring a Chatbot on your company's website.

With this in mind, we've compiled a list of the best AI Chatbots at the time of the writing of this book. We strongly suggest that you try and test each of the most popular ones and see what works best for you.

ChatGPT:
- Uses NLP to understand the context of conversations to provide related and original responses in a human-like conversation.

- Multiple use cases for things like answering questions, ideating and getting inspiration, or generating new content [like a marketing email].
- Improves over time as it has more conversations.

Microsoft Copilot/Bing Chat:
- Uses NLP and ML to understand conversation prompts.
- The compose feature can generate original written content and images, and its powerful search engine capabilities can surface answers from the web.
- It's a conversational tool, so you can continue sending messages until you're satisfied.

Google Gemini/Bard:
- Google's Bard is a multi-use AI Chatbot.
- It's powered by Google's LaMDA [instead of GPT].
- Use it for things like brainstorming and ideation, drafting unique and original content, or getting answers to your questions.
- Connected to Google's website index so it can access information from the internet.

Meta LLaMa:
- Meta's Chatbot is an open source large language [LLM].
- The tool is trained using reinforcement learning from human feedback [RLHF], learning from the preferences and ratings of human AI trainers.

Starting from now, we will refer to these platforms as Chatbots. For a guide on how to sign up to each, please refer to Appendix No 1.

If you're seeking a beginner-friendly, step-by-step guide to using ChatGPT, please refer to Appendix No. 3. This appendix includes access to our report, "Elevate Your Productivity Using ChatGPT," which offers a detailed guide on leveraging ChatGPT to boost efficiency and productivity across a range of professional environments.

As of the book's publication date, the information herein is current and accurate. The Chatbot industry, however, is dynamic, with constant updates and new entrants. While specifics may evolve, our prompts, core strategies and principles discussed in this book are designed to withstand the test of time, offering you a robust framework for navigating this fast-paced landscape.

THE BENEFITS OF USING AI CHATBOTS IN YOUR COACHING, MENTORING AND LEADERSHIP JOURNEY

Navigating the complexities of leadership, coaching, and mentorship has always been a challenging endeavor, akin to a full-time job. The introduction of Chatbots and advanced conversational agents like ChatGPT is revolutionizing this space, offering real-time, AI-generated guidance for professionals striving to excel in these domains.

These AI-driven tools are becoming invaluable assets in the realm of professional development. They offer real-time coaching, behavioral insights, and actionable strategies, which can be a boon for anyone aiming to climb the corporate ladder or make an impact as a leader.

The advantages of integrating Chatbots and the insights from this book into your leadership journey can be broken down into five key areas:

1. **Time-Saving:** The promptness of Chatbots in delivering actionable advice cannot be overstated. From preparing for crucial meetings to formulating impactful leadership principles, these digital assistants can provide timely inputs that significantly shorten your learning curve.
2. **Data-Driven Quality:** Chatbots offer a reliable preliminary layer of advice and strategies, based on extensive data and algorithms. This makes them a formidable starting point for refining your own leadership or coaching plans, tailored to the complexities of your specific environment.
3. **Competitive Advantage:** In an era where tailored solutions are king, Chatbots enable you to customize your leadership or coaching approaches at an unprecedented scale. This functionality allows you to be agile and responsive, traits highly coveted by effective leaders and mentors.
4. **Fresh Perspectives:** Chatbots can serve as a fertile ground for innovative ideas and practices. Leveraging AI's capability to provide data-driven suggestions, you can unearth groundbreaking approaches to leadership that might not be apparent through traditional means.
5. **Self-Empowerment:** The primary goal of this book, when coupled with Chatbots, is to enhance your sense of self-efficacy. As you interact with these technologies, you'll find tailored advice that underscores your unique strengths and challenges, thus fortifying your resolve to excel in leadership and coaching roles.

In a nutshell, combining the AI-enabled capabilities of Chatbots with the in-depth, human-centric insights in this book creates a comprehensive toolkit. This combination promises to redefine and elevate traditional frameworks in leadership, coaching, and mentorship, equipping you with the resources you need to succeed in today's multifaceted professional landscape.

WHAT ARE PROMPTS?

Imagine stepping into a high-stakes negotiation with only half the information—you're likely to miss the mark. Similarly, Chatbots rely on well-crafted prompts to deliver precise and valuable responses.

Prompts serve as the guiding questions, suggestions, or ideas that instruct Chatbots on how and what to respond. But these aren't just any text or phrase; prompts are carefully engineered inputs designed to optimize the Chatbot's output for quality, relevance, and accuracy.

Prompts are suggestions, questions, or ideas for what Chatbots should respond. And for Chatbots to provide a helpful response to their users, they need a thorough prompt with some background information and relevant context. Becoming a solid prompt writer takes time and experience, but there are also some best practices that you can use to see success fairly quickly:

1. **Be precise in your instructions:** when interacting with Chatbots for leadership or coaching tasks, specificity is paramount. Clearly define the tone, scope, and objectives you wish the Chatbot to achieve. For instance, you might say, "Generate a team motivational message that emphasizes the importance of collaboration and aligns with our Q4 targets. Keep the message under 150 words and use a motivational tone."
2. **Integrate contextual information:** the more context you provide, the better Chatbots can tailor their responses. Always include any relevant background information or guidelines. For example, in the case of crafting a message to resolve team conflicts, you may want to append specific issues or arguments that the team is facing.
3. **Segment your interactions:** complex leadership tasks often have multiple components. Break these down into discrete tasks and use individual prompts for each. If you're generating materials for a leadership workshop, you could use separate prompts for the introduction, body, and conclusion segments.
4. **Continuous refinement:** Chatbots provide a valuable starting point but shouldn't replace your own expertise and voice. Use the generated material as a draft that can be further honed and personalized. This ensures that the content aligns with your unique leadership style and the specific needs of your team or mentees.
5. **Employ follow-up prompts:** to get more nuanced advice, use follow-up prompts based on initial outputs. For example, if your first prompt is, "Outline the key principles for effective leadership," a good follow-up could be, "Explain the application of each principle in remote team settings." This sequencing enriches the dialogue and makes the Chatbot's advice more actionable. Check Appendix No 2 for 1100 follow-up prompts you could use, but remember they also need to be tailored to the specific conversation you are having with the Chatbot.

HOW TO USE THIS BOOK?

In the current professional ecosystem, the topics of coaching, mentoring, and leadership are intricate but filled with unprecedented opportunities. This book offers a comprehensive guide for leveraging artificial intelligence, specifically Chatbots, to gain a competitive edge in these sectors. While the content is structured around key frameworks and principles of leadership and coaching, you are encouraged to engage with this book in a non-linear fashion, focusing on areas most relevant to your immediate and long-term objectives.

1. **Optimize your outcomes with our specialized GPT:** We are thrilled to provide exclusive access to "*My Coaching, Mentoring & Leadership Advisor*" GPT, a cutting-edge tool developed using OpenAI's ChatGPT technology. This custom GPT model is specifically designed to offer targeted assistance in leadership, coaching, and mentoring, enhancing your professional journey with AI-driven insights. To maximize its impact, we recommend using this GPT in conjunction with the prompts provided in this book. This synergistic approach will amplify your learning experience, offering a unique blend of expert guidance and personalized AI assistance. To access this GPT, please refer to the following chapter in this book.

2. **Prompt engineering for optimal outcomes:** We advocate for an informed, strategic approach to using the prompts provided in this book. Each prompt is meticulously engineered to serve a specific purpose and is accompanied by its intended goal, a guiding formula, and two illustrative examples. Text highlighted in **bold** and terms enclosed in square brackets [ ] are particularly conducive to customization. We encourage you to not just copy these prompts verbatim but to understand their underlying structure and adapt them to your unique circumstances. The more tailored the prompt, the more relevant and actionable the output will be.

3. **Differentiating complexities for broader utility:** The aim is to offer a broader perspective on how these prompts can be employed and customized. By engaging with a diverse array of prompts, you can develop a nuanced understanding of their underlying mechanisms, thereby gaining the flexibility to tailor them to multiple contexts or objectives.

4. **Integrative strategies for customization:** As you move through this book, you are encouraged to blend different strategies and tools to create customized plans. A well-crafted prompt elicits a higher-quality response; thus, investment in tailoring your inquiries is more than just a recommendation—it's a necessity for meaningful engagement with the book's content.

5. **Ethical considerations and critical thinking:** AI provides valuable insights, but it's crucial to critically evaluate this information. Use Chatbots' advice as a starting point for your strategies, complementing it with further research and ethical considerations. It's essential to remember that while AI can augment decision-making, it can't replace human wisdom.

6. **Communication excellence:** When crafting prompts for Chatbots, aim for clarity and precision. Open-ended questions often lead to more in-depth responses. For a tailored experience, you can also specify the persona or role you want the AI to assume, thereby aligning its feedback with your specific leadership or coaching context.

7. **Target audience, industry, and specificity:** Clearly defining your target audience and industry will enable you to fine-tune the strategies and insights you derive from this book and the accompanying AI resources. Whether you are a leadership consultant, executive coach, or HR professional, audience specificity enhances the utility of the guidance offered.

8. **Getting started with Chatbots:** For those new to the Chatbots platform, we provide a step-by-step guide to get you up and running, empowering you to leverage AI capabilities for your professional development in leadership and coaching.

Here is an overview of the appendices and how they can be integrated into your prompting:

- **Appendix No. 4** - Professions in Mentoring, Coaching, and Leadership: This appendix enumerates key professions that support personal and organizational development through guidance, training, and inspiration. Select the profession most relevant to your current challenge or opportunity to tailor your prompts, ensuring the most pertinent input from the Chatbot.
- **Appendix No. 5** - Specializations in Mentoring, Coaching, and Leadership: This section presents specialized roles within these fields, emphasizing excellence, innovation, and resilience in professional settings. Choose a specialization closely aligned with your specific challenge or opportunity to create effective prompts and receive the most relevant input from the Chatbot.
- **Appendix No. 6** - Tones for Responses from Chatbots: This appendix explores various writing tones you may want Chatbots to use in their responses to your prompts, ensuring alignment with your communication preferences.
- **Appendix No. 7** - Writing Styles for Responses from Chatbots: This section explores a variety of writing styles designed to enhance the clarity and effectiveness of the responses you seek to obtain from Chatbots, ensuring tailored and impactful communication.
- **Appendix No. 8** - Tagging System for Prompt Navigation: This appendix extends beyond the table of contents by offering three tags for each prompt in the book. These tags are carefully selected to assist readers in easily finding the most relevant prompts for their specific challenges or opportunities, ensuring a targeted and efficient use of the book's resources.

By strategically integrating AI tools and best practices, you can enhance not just your personal growth, but also the development of those you coach, mentor, and lead.

MEET "*MY COACHING, MENTORING & LEADERSHIP ADVISOR*" GPT

My Coaching, Mentoring & Leadership Advisor GPT, developed with OpenAI's ChatGPT technology, enhances your interaction with ChatGPT, offering a more tailored and responsive experience.

This custom GPT (Generative Pre-trained Transformer) model is expertly crafted to provide targeted help in leadership, coaching, and mentoring.

As a dynamic Artificial Intelligence companion, it aligns with your unique professional style and needs, providing tailored advice and insights to help navigate your leadership path.

Engaging with this GPT is incredibly intuitive, and simpler than you might expect. Once you access to ChatGPT, you'll be greeted by a user-friendly interface where you can input your questions or prompts.

The GPT responds almost instantly, offering valuable insights and guidance.

Whether you aim to enhance your leadership abilities, improve team dynamics, or foster personal and professional growth, *My Coaching, Mentoring & Leadership Advisor GPT* stands as your gateway to innovative professional development.

Accompanying this section is a screenshot showcasing the user interface you'll encounter when accessing 'My Coaching, Mentoring & Leadership Advisor' GPT. This visual reference provides a clear preview of what to expect, guiding you through your first steps in utilizing this innovative tool.

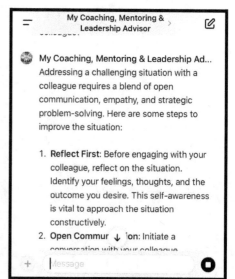

To start your journey towards advanced leadership and coaching skills, and to experience this unique blend of knowledge and technology, please scan this QR code.

Disclaimer: There's a monthly fee for using OpenAI's Plus plan, which you need to access the GPT I created for this book. Wanted to be clear – I don't get any income from OpenAI for suggesting their service. It's all about giving you great tools, and that's why I produced this GPT specifically for the book and for you. As of now, us GPT builders don't get a share of OpenAI's earnings, but if that ever changes – I'll update the disclaimer right away. Mauricio

FREE GOODWILL

Would you consider investing a minute to leave a lasting impression on someone's professional journey? Your experience and insights matter.

Right now, there's a professional, a mentor, or a leader seeking to elevate their capabilities. They're navigating the challenges of leadership, coaching, and perhaps even career transition. Your review could be a pivotal guide for them.

Think of reviews as more than just responses—they're endorsements, collective knowledge, and indicators of reliability. If this book offers you actionable insights or innovative strategies, could you share those experiences through a quick review? By doing so, you contribute to:

- Directing someone to tools and strategies that can heighten their leadership skills.
- Facilitating an individual's capacity to better mentor and coach.
- Enriching someone's perspective, which they might have otherwise overlooked.
- Catalyzing transformation in another's professional path.

By reviewing this book, you contribute to broadening the horizon of effective leadership, mentorship, and coaching for someone else. If you find value in this book, don't hesitate to share it within your network. People remember fondly those who introduced them to beneficial resources.

Your engagement is much appreciated. Thank you for becoming an advocate for impactful leadership and personal development.

Best regards,

Mauricio

PS. To leave your review, please scan this QR code!

Scan the QR code to access our book collection.

TABLE OF CONTENTS

ACCOUNTABILITY

PROMPT No 1

Responsibility - Supportive Identification - Workplace Culture

To gain specific strategies or methods that colleagues can employ to accurately and comprehensively identify individuals who can effectively support them in upholding their accountability and responsibility towards their work, fostering a culture of accountability and responsibility within the workplace.

As a **Leadership Development Consultant**, adopting a **respectful and solution-oriented tone**, could you provide specific strategies or methods that **colleagues** can employ to accurately and comprehensively identify individuals who can effectively support them in **upholding their accountability and responsibility towards their work**? This is particularly relevant given the goal of **fostering a culture of accountability and responsibility within the workplace**.

As a **[profession]**, adopting a **[tone of voice]**, could you provide specific strategies or methods that **[colleagues/team/group]** can employ to accurately and comprehensively identify individuals who can effectively support them in **[contextual challenge/opportunity]**? This is particularly relevant given the goal of **[desired outcome]**.

Example 1: Adopting a clear and concise tone, as a Performance Coach, could you provide specific strategies or methods that a project team can employ to accurately and comprehensively identify individuals who can effectively support them in upholding their accountability and responsibility towards their project tasks? This is particularly relevant given the goal of fostering a culture of accountability and responsibility within the project team.

Example 2: As a Talent Development Specialist, adopting an encouraging and collaborative tone, could you provide specific strategies or methods that colleagues in a marketing department can employ to accurately and comprehensively identify individuals who can effectively support them in upholding their accountability and responsibility towards their marketing campaigns? This is particularly relevant given the goal of fostering a culture of accountability and responsibility within the marketing department.

PROMPT No 2

Accountability - Relationships - Collaboration

To understand how to leverage peer relationships as a tool for enhancing accountability within a team.

In the context of a **collaborative work environment**, as a **Professional Coach** and in a **supportive and encouraging tone**, could you explain how **my team** could utilize their work relationships with their **peers** as a measure of **accountability**?

In the context of **[contextual challenge/opportunity]**, as a **[profession]** and in a **[tone of voice]**, could you explain how **[I/Name/Role]**'s team could utilize their work relationships with their **[peers/colleagues]** as a measure of **[desired outcome]?**

Example 1: In the context of a collaborative project, as a Professional Coach and in a supportive tone, could you explain how my business partners could utilize their work relationships with their peers as a measure of accountability?

Example 2: As a Leadership Consultant, in an encouraging tone, could you explain how my team could utilize their work relationships with their colleagues as a measure of accountability, especially in the context of a remote working environment?

ACTION

PROMPT No 3

Team Resilience - Problem-Solving - Supportive Leadership

To gain specific and practical strategies or actions that can be adopted to greatly improve support and assistance to the team when they encounter a problem, with the aim of enhancing team resilience and problem-solving capabilities.

As a **Leadership Coach**, adopting a **supportive and solution-oriented tone**, could you please provide specific and practical strategies or actions that I can adopt to greatly improve my support and assistance to **my team** when they encounter a problem? Your response should include detailed and comprehensive suggestions that **will help me enhance my effectiveness in providing assistance and support during challenging situations**. This is particularly relevant given the goal of **improving team resilience and problem-solving capabilities**.

As a **[profession]**, adopting a **[tone of voice]**, could you please provide specific and practical strategies or actions that I can adopt to greatly improve my support and assistance to **[my/their] [team/group/department]** when they encounter a problem? Your response should include detailed and comprehensive suggestions that **[contextual challenge/opportunity]**. This is particularly relevant given the goal of **[desired outcome]**.

Example 1: As a Team Coach, adopting an encouraging and patient tone, could you please provide specific and practical strategies or actions that I can adopt to greatly improve my support and assistance to the sales department when they encounter a problem? Your response should include detailed and comprehensive suggestions that will help me enhance my effectiveness in providing assistance and support during challenging situations. This is

Team Resilience - Problem-Solving - Supportive Leadership

particularly relevant given the goal of improving department resilience and problem-solving capabilities.

Example 2: Adopting a respectful and collaborative tone, as a Leadership Development Consultant, could you please provide specific and practical strategies or actions that I can adopt to greatly improve my support and assistance to my project team when they encounter a problem? Your response should include detailed and comprehensive suggestions that will help me enhance my effectiveness in providing assistance and support during challenging situations. This is particularly relevant given the goal of improving team resilience and problem-solving capabilities within the project.

PROMPT No 4

Task Prioritization - Team Autonomy - Efficiency Enhancement

To gain a comprehensive understanding of the procedures and strategies that can be utilized by the team to autonomously identify and prioritize crucial tasks or projects, with the aim of enhancing team autonomy and efficiency in task prioritization.

As a **Performance Coach**, adopting a **clear and concise tone**, could you please provide a comprehensive explanation of the step-by-step procedures and effective strategies that **my team** can utilize to **autonomously identify and prioritize the utmost crucial tasks or projects that demand their immediate attention**? This is particularly relevant given the goal of **enhancing team autonomy and efficiency in task prioritization**.

As a **[profession]**, adopting a **[tone of voice]**, could you please provide a comprehensive explanation of the step-by-step procedures and effective strategies that **[my/their]** **[team/group/department]** can utilize to **[contextual challenge/opportunity]**? This is particularly relevant given the goal of **[desired outcome]**.

Example 1: As a Talent Development Specialist, adopting an encouraging and professional tone, could you please provide a comprehensive explanation of the step-by-step procedures and effective strategies that my marketing team can utilize to autonomously identify and prioritize the utmost crucial tasks or projects that demand their immediate attention? This is particularly relevant given the goal of enhancing team autonomy and efficiency in task prioritization.

Example 2: Adopting a respectful and solution-oriented tone, as a Leadership Development Consultant, could you please provide a comprehensive explanation of the step-by-step procedures and effective strategies that the HR department can utilize to autonomously identify and prioritize the utmost crucial tasks or projects that demand their immediate attention? This is particularly relevant given the goal of enhancing department autonomy and efficiency in task prioritization.

PROMPT No 5

Goal Achievement - Ambition Cultivation - Success Strategies

To gain a detailed and comprehensive understanding of specific strategies a team can explore and implement to successfully attain the goals and achievements they have envisioned for their future, fostering a culture of ambition and success.

Given the aspiration of **attaining envisioned future goals**, as a **Career Coach** and in an **optimistic and clear tone**, could you provide a detailed and comprehensive response on specific strategies **my team** can explore and implement?

Given the aspiration of **[contextual challenge/opportunity]**, as a **[profession]** and in a **[tone of voice]**, could you provide a detailed and comprehensive response on specific strategies **[I/Name/Role]**'s **[team/group/department]** can explore and implement?

Example 1: Given the aspiration of attaining envisioned future goals in a dynamic startup environment, as a Business Coach and in an energetic and motivating tone, could you provide a detailed and comprehensive response on specific strategies a startup team can explore and implement?

Example 2: As a Leadership Development Facilitator, in an inspiring and enthusiastic tone, could you provide a detailed and comprehensive response on specific strategies my engineering team can explore and implement to successfully attain the goals and achievements they have envisioned for their future? This advice is particularly relevant given the aspiration of driving innovation in a competitive tech industry.

AWARENESS

PROMPT No 6

Resource Optimization - Allocation Efficiency - Task Management

To gain specific details that will enable the identification of areas where a team is either allocating too many resources or not enough in their tasks, enhancing resource optimization and team performance.

In the context of **optimizing resource allocation**, as a **Management Consultant** and in a **clear and concise tone**, could you furnish **me** with specific details that will enable **me** to determine the areas where **my team** is either allocating too many resources or not enough in their tasks?

In the context of **[contextual challenge/opportunity]**, as a **[profession]** and in a **[tone of voice]**, could you furnish **[I/Name/Role]** with specific details that will enable

[me/them] to determine the areas where **[my/their]** **[team/group/department]** is either allocating too many resources or not enough in their tasks?

Examples

Example 1: In the context of optimizing resource allocation in a manufacturing environment, as an Organizational Development Consultant and in a professional and solution-oriented tone, could you furnish a plant manager with specific details that will enable them to determine the areas where their team is either allocating too many resources or not enough in their tasks?

Example 2: As a Performance Coach, in a respectful and supportive tone, could you furnish me with specific details that will enable me to determine the areas where my customer service team is either allocating too many resources or not enough in their tasks? This advice is particularly relevant in the context of optimizing resource allocation to improve customer satisfaction.

PROMPT No 7

Tags

Positive Mindset - Motivation Maintenance - Supportive Leadership

Goal

To gain a detailed understanding of specific approaches, techniques, or actions that can be adopted to provide effective support and guidance to a team, with the aim of preventing any decrease in their motivation and attitude, and ensuring they consistently maintain a positive mindset.

Prompt

As a **Leadership Coach**, adopting a **motivational and supportive tone**, could you provide **me** with specific approaches, techniques, or actions that **I** can adopt to provide effective support and guidance to my **team**? This is particularly relevant given the goal of **preventing any decrease in their motivation and attitude, and ensuring they consistently maintain a positive mindset**.

Formula

As a **[profession]**, adopting a **[tone of voice]**, could you provide **[me/Name/Role]** with specific approaches, techniques, or actions that **[I/Name/Role]** can adopt to provide effective support and guidance to **[my/their]** **[team/group/department]**? This is particularly relevant given the goal of **[desired outcome]**.

Examples

Example 1: As a Team Development Specialist, adopting an encouraging and positive tone, could you provide me with specific approaches, techniques, or actions that I can adopt to provide effective support and guidance to my sales team? This is particularly relevant given the goal of preventing any decrease in their motivation and attitude, and ensuring they consistently maintain a positive mindset.

Example 2: As a Human Resources Consultant, adopting a respectful and understanding tone, could you provide the department head with specific approaches, techniques, or actions that they can adopt to provide effective support and guidance to their IT department? This is particularly relevant given the goal of preventing any decrease in their motivation and attitude, and ensuring they consistently maintain a positive mindset.

PROMPT No 8

Tags

Ideal Self - Self-Awareness - Professional Growth

Goal

To gain insights on specific actions to assist a team in recognizing the differences between their ideal and actual selves, fostering self-awareness and personal and professional growth.

Prompt

Considering the importance of **self-awareness in personal and professional growth**, as an **Executive Coach** and in an **empathetic and respectful tone**, could you suggest specific actions **I** can take to assist **my team** in **recognizing the differences between their ideal and actual selves**?

Formula

Considering the importance of **[contextual challenge/opportunity]**, as a **[profession]** and in a **[tone of voice]**, could you suggest specific actions **[I/Name/Role]** can take to assist **[my/their]** **[team/group/department]** in **[desired outcome]**?

Examples

Example 1: Considering the importance of self-awareness in personal and professional growth, as a Career Coach and in a supportive and patient tone, could you suggest specific actions a department head can take to assist their faculty in recognizing the differences between their ideal and actual selves?

Example 2: As a Leadership Development Facilitator, in an open-minded and considerate tone, could you suggest specific actions I can take to assist my sales team in recognizing the differences between their ideal and actual selves? This advice is particularly relevant considering the importance of self-awareness in achieving sales targets.

PROMPT No 9

Tags

Questioning - Insight - Understanding

Goal

To acquire effective strategies for developing questioning skills that can lead to a deeper understanding of team members' roles, challenges, and opportunities, thereby increasing influence within the team and contributing to the organization's success.

Prompt

As a **Leadership Development Consultant**, adopting a **supportive and insightful tone**, could you provide me with strategies to **enhance my questioning skills**? I am particularly interested in **asking more impactful and insightful questions to my team members about the challenges they face and the opportunities they encounter**. My ultimate goal is to **gain a comprehensive understanding of their roles and actively contribute to the overall success of our organization**.

Formula

As a **[profession]**, adopting a **[tone of voice]**, could you provide me with strategies to enhance my **[desired skill]**? I am particularly interested in **[specific area of interest]**. My ultimate goal is to **[desired outcome]**.

Examples

Example 1: As a Communication Skills Trainer, adopting a clear and concise tone, could you provide me with strategies to enhance my questioning skills? I am particularly interested in asking more impactful and insightful questions to my project team about the challenges they face and the opportunities they encounter. My ultimate goal is to gain a comprehensive understanding of their roles and actively contribute to the overall success of our project.

Example 2: As a Team Coach, adopting an encouraging and professional tone, could you provide me with strategies to enhance my questioning skills? I am particularly interested in asking more impactful and insightful questions to my sales team about the challenges they face and the opportunities they encounter. My ultimate goal is to gain a comprehensive understanding of their roles and actively contribute to the overall success of our sales targets.

PROMPT No 10

Tags

Mindset - Positive - Conversion

Goal

To gain insights on specific and practical strategies and techniques that can be utilized to successfully identify and convert the negative and unproductive mindset displayed by a team into a positive and productive one.

Prompt

As a **Leadership Development Consultant**, adopting a **supportive and encouraging tone**, could you provide specific and practical strategies and techniques that can be utilized to **successfully identify and convert the negative and unproductive mindset** displayed by my team into a **positive and productive one**?

Formula

As a **[profession]**, adopting a **[tone of voice]**, could you provide specific and practical strategies and techniques that can be utilized to **[contextual challenge/opportunity]** displayed by **[my/their] [team/group/department]** into a **[contextual challenge/opportunity]**?

Examples

Example 1: As a Team Coach, adopting a supportive and encouraging tone, could you provide specific and practical strategies and techniques that can be utilized to successfully identify and convert the negative and unproductive mindset displayed by my construction team into a positive and productive one?

Example 2: As a Management Consultant, adopting a supportive and encouraging tone, could you provide specific and practical strategies and techniques that can be utilized to successfully identify and convert the negative and unproductive mindset displayed by the procurement department into a positive and productive one?

PROMPT No 11

Tags

Barriers - Detection - Progress

Goal

To gain a comprehensive understanding of practical strategies that can be used to identify and address both internal and external barriers that could potentially obstruct the actions and progress of a team.

As a **Leadership Development Consultant**, adopting a **solution-oriented and proactive tone**, could you provide concrete and detailed approaches that can be utilized to accurately **detect and tackle internal as well as external barriers** that could hinder **the actions and advancement of my team** in an efficient manner?

Formula

As a **[profession]**, adopting a **[tone of voice]**, could you provide **[specific/detailed/concrete]** approaches that can be utilized to accurately **[desired outcome]** that could hinder **[contextual challenge/opportunity]** in an efficient manner?

Examples

Example 1: As a Management Consultant, adopting a strategic and proactive tone, could you provide specific approaches that can be utilized to accurately detect and tackle internal as well as external barriers that could hinder the actions and advancement of my marketing team in an efficient manner?

Example 2: As a Team Coach, adopting a solution-oriented and proactive tone, could you provide detailed approaches that can be utilized to accurately detect and tackle internal as well as external barriers that could hinder the actions and advancement of my sales team in an efficient manner?

BELIEF

PROMPT No 12

Tags

Hindrance - Development - Mindset

Goal

To gain insights on improving the approach to discussing beliefs that hinder the team's progress and to learn strategies to assist the team in developing empowering beliefs, fostering a positive mindset and improved performance.

Prompt

As a **Leadership Development Consultant**, adopting a **supportive and constructive tone**, could you suggest specific steps I can take to enhance **my** approach when addressing the beliefs that are hindering **my team** from reaching their **goals or fulfilling their commitments**? Furthermore, could you recommend strategies **I** can implement to help them develop their own empowering beliefs? This is particularly relevant given the goal of **fostering a positive mindset and improved performance**.

Formula

As a **[profession]**, adopting a **[tone of voice]**, could you suggest specific steps **[I/Name/Role]** can take to enhance **[my/their]** approach when addressing the beliefs that are hindering **[my/their]** **[team/group/department]** from reaching their **[contextual challenge/opportunity]**? Furthermore, could you recommend strategies **[I/Name/Role]** can implement to help them develop their own empowering beliefs? This is particularly relevant given the goal of **[desired outcome]**.

Examples

Example 1: As a Team Coach, adopting a compassionate and understanding tone, could you suggest specific steps a department head can take to enhance their approach when addressing the beliefs that are hindering their faculty from reaching their academic goals or fulfilling their commitments? Furthermore, could you recommend strategies they can implement to help them develop their own empowering beliefs? This is particularly relevant given the goal of fostering a positive mindset and improved academic performance.

Example 2: As a Human Resources (HR) Consultant, adopting a respectful and professional tone, could you suggest specific steps I can take to enhance my approach when addressing the beliefs that are hindering my project team from reaching their project goals or fulfilling their commitments? Furthermore, could you recommend strategies I can implement to help them develop their own empowering beliefs? This is particularly relevant given the goal of fostering a positive mindset and improved project performance.

PROMPT No 13

Tags

Assessment - Engagement - Strategies

Goal

To gain insights on the most effective methods or strategies to assess the extent to which my team's beliefs regarding a particular issue or problem are beneficial for them.

Prompt

As a **Leadership Development Consultant**, adopting a **supportive and analytical tone,** could you provide insights on the most effective methods or strategies to assess the extent to which **my team**'s beliefs regarding **their lack of engagement** are beneficial for them?

Formula

As a **[profession]**, adopting a **[tone of voice]**, could you provide insights on the most effective methods or strategies to assess the extent to which **[my/their]** **[team/group/department]**'s beliefs regarding **[particular issue or problem]** are beneficial for them?

Examples

Example 1: As a Team Coach, adopting a collaborative and respectful tone, could you provide insights on the most effective methods or strategies to assess the extent to which my project team's beliefs regarding a project delay are beneficial for them?

Example 2: Adopting a supportive and analytical tone, as a Human Resources (HR) Consultant, could you provide insights on the most effective methods or strategies to assess the extent to which a department's beliefs regarding a change in management are beneficial for them?

PROMPT No 14

Tags

Core-Values - Behavior -Professionalism

Goal

To gain insights on identifying the core values that guide team members in their professional journeys and to understand how these beliefs shape their behaviors and choices within the workplace.

Prompt

As a **Leadership Development Consultant**, adopting a **supportive and respectful tone**, could you help **me** identify the specific core values that **my team members** uphold as **guiding principles in their professional journeys**? Additionally, could you explain how these beliefs **shape and impact their behaviors and choices within the workplace**?

As a **[profession]**, adopting a **[tone of voice]**, could you help **[me/Name/Role]** identify the specific core values that **[my/their]** **[team/group/department]** uphold as **[contextual challenge/opportunity]**? Additionally, could you explain how these beliefs **[contextual challenge/opportunity]**?

Example 1: As a Team Coach, adopting an empathetic and understanding tone, could you help a department head identify the specific core values that their IT team uphold as guiding principles in their professional journeys? Additionally, could you explain how these beliefs shape and impact their behaviors and choices within the high-stress environment of their IT projects?

Example 2: As a Human Resources (HR) Consultant, adopting a clear and concise tone, could you help me identify the specific core values that my accounting team uphold as guiding principles in their professional journeys? Additionally, could you explain how these beliefs shape and impact their behaviors and choices within the competitive accounting environment?

PROMPT No 15

Awareness - Outcomes - Decision-Making

To gain specific strategies, practices, or tools that can be utilized to improve the team's awareness and to ensure that the team has a thorough understanding of the potential outcomes and impacts of their decisions and actions, fostering a more informed and conscious decision-making process within the team.

As a **Leadership Development Consultant**, adopting an **informative and detailed tone**, could you provide specific strategies, practices, or tools that can be utilized to improve **my team's awareness**? Additionally, how can we ensure that **my team** has a thorough understanding of the **potential outcomes and impacts of our decisions and actions**? Please provide detailed and comprehensive suggestions for each question separately.

As a **[profession]**, adopting a **[tone of voice]**, could you provide specific strategies, practices, or tools that can be utilized to improve **[my/their]** **[team/group/department's]** **[desired outcome]**? Additionally, how can we ensure that **[my/their]** **[team/group/department]** has a thorough understanding of the **[contextual challenge/opportunity]**? Please provide detailed and comprehensive suggestions for each question separately.

Example 1: As a Team Coach, adopting a clear and concise tone, could you provide specific strategies, practices, or tools that can be utilized to improve my project team's awareness? Additionally, how can we ensure that my project team has a thorough understanding of the potential outcomes and impacts of our decisions and actions? Please provide detailed and comprehensive suggestions for each question separately.

Example 2: As an Organizational Development Specialist, adopting a professional and detailed tone, could you provide specific strategies, practices, or tools that can be utilized to improve the sales department's awareness? Additionally, how can we ensure that the sales department has a thorough understanding of the potential outcomes and impacts of our decisions and actions? Please provide detailed and comprehensive suggestions for each question separately.

PROMPT No 16

Tags

Motivation - Analysis - Evidence

Goal

To gain a detailed understanding of the most effective and specific strategies or methods that can be employed to motivate and inspire a team to conduct a comprehensive and meticulous analysis of evidence and criteria when evaluating a decision or course of action, fostering informed decision-making and effective problem-solving within the team.

Prompt

As a **Leadership Development Consultant**, adopting a **motivational and informative tone**, could you provide the most effective and specific strategies or methods that can be employed to **motivate and inspire my team to conduct a comprehensive and meticulous analysis of evidence and criteria when evaluating a decision or course of action**? This is particularly relevant given the goal of fostering informed decision-making and effective problem-solving within the team.

Formula

As a **[profession]**, adopting a **[tone of voice]**, could you provide the most effective and specific strategies or methods that can be employed to **[contextual challenge/opportunity] [my/their] [team/group/department] [contextual challenge/opportunity]**? This is particularly relevant given the goal of **[desired outcome]**.

Examples

Example 1: As a Team Coach, adopting an encouraging and informative tone, could you provide the most effective and specific strategies or methods that can be employed to motivate and inspire my project team to conduct a comprehensive and meticulous analysis of evidence and criteria when evaluating a decision or course of action? This is particularly relevant given the goal of fostering informed decision-making and effective problem-solving within the project team.

Example 2: As a Management Consultant, adopting a motivational and informative tone, could you provide the most effective and specific strategies or methods that can be employed to motivate and inspire a department head's team to conduct a comprehensive and meticulous analysis of evidence and criteria when evaluating a decision or course of action? This is particularly relevant given the goal of fostering informed decision-making and effective problem-solving within the department.

CHALLENGE

PROMPT No 17

Innovation - Encouragement - Challenges

To gain specific tactics or methods to inspire and encourage team members to step out of their comfort zones and take on new challenges, fostering a culture of innovation and growth.

Given the goal of **inspiring team members to step out of their comfort zones and take on new challenges**, as a **Leadership Coach** and in an **encouraging and motivational tone**, could you outline specific tactics or methods **I** can employ?

Given the goal of **[contextual challenge/opportunity]**, as a **[profession]** and in a **[tone of voice]**, could you outline specific tactics or methods **[I/Name/Role]** can employ?

Example 1: Given the goal of inspiring team members to step out of their comfort zones and take on new challenges in a startup environment, as a Performance Coach and in an enthusiastic and supportive tone, could you outline specific tactics or methods a startup founder can employ?

Example 2: As a Talent Development Specialist, in an inspirational and empowering tone, could you outline specific tactics or methods I can employ to inspire and encourage members of my marketing team to step out of their comfort zones and take on new challenges? This advice is particularly relevant given the goal of fostering a culture of innovation and growth.

PROMPT No 18

Self-awareness - Decision-Making - Beliefs

To foster self-awareness and improve decision-making skills among employees.

As a **Leadership Development Coach**, with a focus on **fostering self-awareness and improving decision-making skills** among employees, I would like to request a comprehensive and detailed explanation on **how personal beliefs have a significant impact on decision-making processes in the workplace**. It would be greatly appreciated if you could adopt a **reflective and instructive tone** while addressing this topic. Additionally, I would like you to **identify specific ways in which these personal beliefs shape choices and guide actions in professional settings**.

As a **[profession]**, with a focus on **[desired outcome]**, I would like to request a comprehensive and detailed explanation on **[topic]**. It would be greatly appreciated if you could adopt a **[tone of voice]** while addressing this topic. Additionally, I would like you to **[additional request]**.

Example 1: As a Human Resources Manager, with a focus on improving employee engagement and satisfaction, I would like to request a comprehensive and detailed explanation on how workplace culture influences employee morale. It would be greatly appreciated if you could adopt a factual and informative tone while addressing this topic. Additionally, I would like you to provide specific examples of companies that have successfully improved their workplace culture.

Example 2: As a Marketing Director, with a focus on increasing brand awareness and customer loyalty, I would like to request a comprehensive and detailed explanation on how social media marketing strategies can be optimized for better reach and engagement. It would be greatly appreciated if you could adopt a practical and insightful tone while addressing this topic. Additionally, I would like you to suggest some innovative social media marketing tactics that can be implemented.

PROMPT No 19

Tags

Data - Relevance - Strategies

Goal

To gain specific actions and strategies that can be employed to assist a team in identifying the most relevant and reliable data sources that can effectively support or challenge their assumptions.

Prompt

As a **Data Analyst**, adopting a **clear and concise tone**, could you provide specific actions and strategies that **I** can employ to assist **my team** in **identifying the most relevant and reliable data sources** that can effectively **support or challenge their assumptions**?

Formula

As a **[profession]**, adopting a **[tone of voice]**, could you provide specific actions and strategies that **[I/Name/Role]** can employ to assist **[my/their]** **[team/group/department]** in **[desired outcome]** that can effectively **[contextual challenge/opportunity]**?

Examples

Example 1: As a Business Intelligence Consultant, adopting a solution-oriented tone, could you provide specific actions and strategies that a project manager can employ to assist their project team in identifying the most relevant and reliable data sources that can effectively support or challenge their project assumptions?

Example 2: As a Data Science Advisor, adopting a professional and instructive tone, could you provide specific actions and strategies that I can employ to assist my marketing team in identifying the most relevant and reliable data sources that can effectively support or challenge their market assumptions?

PROMPT No 20

Tags

Problem-Solving - Cultivation - Empowerment

Goal

To gain specific strategies or activities that can be implemented to cultivate a problem-solving mindset within a team, enabling them to effectively confront and surmount any challenges they encounter.

Prompt

As a **Leadership Development Consultant**, adopting an **empowering and solution-oriented tone**, could you recommend specific strategies or activities that **I** can implement to cultivate a **problem-solving mindset** in **my team**, enabling them to effectively **confront and surmount any challenges they encounter**?

Formula

As a **[profession]**, adopting a **[tone of voice]**, could you recommend specific strategies or activities that **[I/Name/Role]** can implement to cultivate a **[desired outcome]** in **[my/their]** **[team/group/department]**, enabling them to effectively **[contextual challenge/opportunity]**?

Examples

Example 1: As a Team Coach, adopting a supportive and encouraging tone, could you recommend specific strategies or activities that a department head can implement to cultivate a problem-solving mindset in their faculty, enabling them to effectively confront and surmount any academic challenges they encounter?

Example 2: As a Performance Coach, adopting a motivational and solution-oriented tone, could you recommend specific strategies or activities that I can implement to cultivate a problem-solving mindset in my project team, enabling them to effectively confront and surmount any project-related challenges they encounter?

PROMPT No 21

Tags

Team-Motivation - Leadership - Empowerment

Goal

To gain specific and practical strategies, methods, and approaches to successfully motivate and empower a team to overcome any internal barriers or doubts, fostering an environment that compels decisive action and the accomplishment of shared objectives.

Prompt

As a **Leadership Coach**, adopting an **empowering and optimistic tone**, could you provide specific and practical strategies, methods, and approaches that **I** can employ to successfully **motivate and empower my team to overcome any internal barriers or doubts they may possess**? I aim to **foster an environment that compels them to take decisive action and ultimately accomplish our shared objectives**.

Formula

As a **[profession]**, adopting a **[tone of voice]**, could you provide specific and practical strategies, methods, and approaches that **[I/Name/Role]** can employ to successfully **[contextual challenge/opportunity]** **[my/their]** **[team/group/department]**? I aim to **[desired outcome]**.

Examples

Example 1: As a Performance Coach, adopting an energetic and motivational tone, could you provide specific and practical strategies, methods, and approaches that a department head can employ to successfully motivate and empower their faculty to overcome any internal barriers or doubts they may possess? They aim to foster an environment that compels decisive action and ultimately accomplish their academic objectives.

Example 2: As a Team Coach, adopting an enthusiastic and optimistic tone, could you provide specific and practical strategies, methods, and approaches that I can employ to successfully motivate and empower my project team to overcome any internal barriers or doubts they may possess? I aim to foster an environment that compels decisive action and ultimately accomplish our project objectives.

PROMPT No 110

Comfort-Zone - Performance - Team-Dynamics

To gain specific strategies or methods to accurately determine the boundaries of a team's comfort zone, fostering an understanding of team dynamics and enabling the expansion of comfort zones for enhanced performance

As a **Performance Coach**, adopting a **respectful and professional tone**, could you suggest specific strategies or methods that **I** can use to accurately determine the **boundaries of my team's comfort zone**? This is particularly relevant given the goal of **understanding and expanding comfort zones for enhanced performance**.

As a **[profession]**, adopting a **[tone of voice]**, could you suggest specific strategies or methods that **[I/Name/Role]** can use to accurately determine the **[contextual challenge/opportunity]** of **[my/their]** **[team/group/department]**? This is particularly relevant given the goal of **[desired outcome]**.

Example 1: Adopting a clear and concise tone, as a Leadership Development Consultant, could you suggest specific strategies or methods that a department head can use to accurately determine the boundaries of their faculty's comfort zone? This is particularly relevant given the goal of understanding and expanding comfort zones for enhanced academic performance.

Example 2: As a Team Coach, adopting an empathetic and supportive tone, could you suggest specific strategies or methods that I can use to accurately determine the boundaries of my project team's comfort zone? This is particularly relevant given the goal of understanding and expanding comfort zones for enhanced project outcomes.

PROMPT No 22

Productive-Discussion - Impediment - Insight

To gain specific strategies and approaches to enhance the ability to have productive and insightful discussions with a team about the factors that have impeded their progress or work towards achieving their goals.

As a **Leadership Development Consultant**, adopting a **supportive and understanding tone**, could you provide specific strategies and approaches that **I** can employ to enhance **my** ability to have productive and insightful discussions with **my team** about the factors that have impeded their **progress or work towards achieving their goals**?

As a **[profession]**, adopting a **[tone of voice]**, could you provide specific strategies and approaches that **[I/Name/Role]** can employ to enhance **[my/their]** ability to have productive and insightful discussions with **[my/their]** **[team/group/department]** about the factors that have impeded their **[contextual challenge/opportunity]**?

Example 1: As a Team Coach, adopting a patient and empathetic tone, could you provide specific strategies and approaches that a department head can employ to enhance their ability to have productive and insightful discussions with their faculty about the factors that have impeded their academic progress or work towards achieving their teaching goals? **Example 2:** As a Business Coach, adopting a respectful and professional tone, could you provide specific strategies and approaches that I can employ to enhance my ability to have productive and insightful discussions with my project team about the factors that have impeded their project progress or work towards achieving their project goals?

CHANGE

PROMPT No 23

Change-Management - Innovation - Adaptability

To gain specific methods and strategies that leaders can employ to effectively anticipate and navigate rapid changes and innovations in their industry, while also ensuring their team is well-prepared and adaptable.

As a **Change Management Consultant**, adopting a **proactive and strategic tone**, could you provide specific methods and strategies that **I**, as a leader, can employ to effectively anticipate and navigate **rapid changes and innovations** in **my** industry, while also ensuring **my team** is **well-prepared and adaptable**? This is particularly relevant given the **dynamic nature of our industry**.

As a **[profession]**, adopting a **[tone of voice]**, could you provide specific methods and strategies that **[I/Name/Role]**, as a leader, can employ to effectively anticipate and navigate **[contextual challenge/opportunity]** in **[my/their]** industry, while also ensuring **[my/their]** **[team/group/department]** is **[desired outcome]**? This is particularly relevant given the **[contextual challenge/opportunity]**.

Example 1: As a Business Strategist, adopting a forward-thinking and analytical tone, could you provide specific methods and strategies that a department head can employ to effectively anticipate and navigate rapid changes and innovations in the tech industry, while also ensuring their IT team is well-prepared and adaptable? This is particularly relevant given the dynamic nature of the tech industry.

Example 2: As a Leadership Development Consultant, adopting a proactive and strategic tone, could you provide specific methods and strategies that I, as a project manager, can employ to effectively anticipate and navigate rapid changes and innovations in the construction industry, while also ensuring my project team is well-prepared and adaptable? This is particularly relevant given the dynamic nature of the construction industry.

PROMPT No 24

Forward-Thinking - Impact - Strategy

To gain specific strategies or tools to effectively engage in a discussion with a team about how their current work will impact and shape future outcomes, fostering a forward-thinking mindset within the team.

As a **Leadership Development Consultant**, adopting a **forward-thinking and engaging tone**, could you provide specific strategies or tools that **I** can utilize to effectively engage in a discussion with **my team** about how their current work will **impact and shape future outcomes**? This is particularly relevant given the goal of **fostering a forward-thinking mindset within the team**.

As a **[profession]**, adopting a **[tone of voice]**, could you provide specific strategies or tools that **[I/Name/Role]** can utilize to effectively engage in a discussion with **[my/their]** **[team/group/department]** about how their current work will **[contextual challenge/opportunity]**? This is particularly relevant given the goal of **[desired outcome]**.

Example 1: As a Team Coach, adopting a proactive and engaging tone, could you provide specific strategies or tools that a department head can utilize to effectively engage in a discussion with their faculty about how their current teaching methods will impact and shape future academic outcomes? This is particularly relevant given the goal of fostering a forward-thinking mindset within the faculty.

Example 2: As a Business Coach, adopting a strategic and engaging tone, could you provide specific strategies or tools that I can utilize to effectively engage in a discussion with my project team about how their current project management practices will impact and shape future project outcomes? This is particularly relevant given the goal of fostering a forward-thinking mindset within the project team.

PROMPT No 25

Prioritization - Decision-Making - Task-Management

To obtain a list of criteria that a team should consider when deciding which tasks or projects to let go of in order to prioritize effectively.

In the context of a **team needing to prioritize and let go of certain tasks or projects**, as a **performance management specialist** and in a **clear and concise tone**, could you list the criteria **my team** needs to consider when **making these decisions**?

In the context of **[contextual challenge/opportunity]**, as a **[profession]** and in a **[tone of voice]**, could you list the criteria **[I/Name/Role]'s [team/group/department]** needs to consider when **[desired outcome]**?

Example 1: In the context of a project team needing to prioritize tasks due to limited resources, as a project management consultant and in a solution-oriented tone, could you list the criteria the team needs to consider when deciding which tasks to let go of?

Example 2: As a time management specialist and in a professional and friendly tone, could you list the criteria my team needs to consider when selecting the tasks they need to let go of, especially in the context of a high workload environment?

COMMITMENT

ROMPT No 26

Influence - Commitment - Goal-Orientation

To gain strategies on how to effectively influence a team to commit to their goals, enhancing their performance and productivity.

In the context of **fostering a goal-oriented team culture**, as a **leadership coach** and in **an inspiring and motivating tone**, could you advise on how **I** could influence **my team** to commit themselves to achieving their **goals**?

In the context of **[contextual challenge/opportunity]**, as a **[profession]** and in a **[tone of voice]**, could you advise on how **[I/Name/Role]** could influence **[my/their] [team/group/department]** to commit themselves to achieving their **[goals/targets/objectives]**?

Example 1: In the context of a competitive sales environment, as a performance coach and in an enthusiastic and energetic tone, could you advise on how a sales manager could influence their team to commit themselves to achieving their sales targets?

Example 2: As a team coach, in a supportive and encouraging tone, could you advise on how I could influence my project team to commit themselves to achieving their project deliverables, particularly in the context of tight deadlines?

Tags

Composure - Support - Well-being

Goal

To an actionable framework for assisting team members in managing personal issues while maintaining professional composure, thereby fostering a supportive work environment and enhancing overall team well-being.

Prompt

As an **Employee Relations Manager** specializing in the **healthcare sector**, could you **delineate specific methods** I can **employ** to **assist** my team in **managing personal issues** while **maintaining composure** at work? Include **evidence-based practices, psychological theories, and real-world case studies**. Let's think about this step by step. Write using an **empathetic** tone and a **respectful** writing style.

Formula

As an **[Employee Relations Manager/HR Specialist/Well-being Coordinator]** specializing in the **[healthcare/technology/finance]** sector, could you **[delineate/suggest/elaborate on]** **[specific methods/strategies/approaches]** I can **[employ/use/implement]** to **[assist/support/guide]** my team in **[managing/handling/addressing]** **[personal issues/life challenges/emotional struggles]** while **[maintaining/keeping/sustaining]** **[composure/professionalism/equanimity]** at work? Include **[evidence-based practices/empirical data]**, **[psychological theories/behavioral models]**, and **[real-world case studies/practical examples]**. Let's **[think about this step by step/methodically dissect each component]**. Write using a **[empathetic/respectful/compassionate]** tone and a **[respectful/considerate/tactful]** writing style.

Examples

Example 1: As a Well-being Coordinator specializing in the technology sector, could you suggest strategies I can use to support my team in handling life challenges while keeping professionalism at work? Include empirical data, behavioral models, and practical examples. Let's carefully evaluate each segment. Write using an empathetic tone and a considerate writing style.

Example 2: As an HR Specialist specializing in the finance sector, could you elaborate on approaches I can implement to guide my team in addressing emotional struggles while sustaining equanimity at work? Include evidence-based practices, psychological theories, and real-world case studies. Let's systematically explore each facet. Write using a respectful tone and a tactful writing style.

CREATIVITY

PROMPT No 28

Tags

Creativity - Problem-Solving - Innovation

Goal

To gain insights on ways to foster and unleash creativity within a team, enhancing their innovation and problem-solving capabilities.

In the context of **fostering innovation in a team**, as a **leadership development facilitator** and in an **empowering and inspirational tone**, could you explain ways **I** can typically unleash the **creativity of my team**?

In the context of **[contextual challenge/opportunity]**, as a **[profession]** and in a **[tone of voice]**, could you explain ways **[I/Name/Role]** can typically unleash the **[desired outcome]** of **[my/their] [team/group/department]**?

Example 1: In the context of a new product development project, as a talent development specialist and in an enthusiastic and energetic tone, could you explain ways a project manager can typically unleash the creativity of their team?

Example 2: As a creative director, in an optimistic and encouraging tone, could you explain ways I can typically unleash the creativity of my design team, especially in the context of creating a new advertising campaign?

PROMPT No 29

Creativity - Enhancement - Responsibilities

To gain specific strategies or approaches that can be implemented to effectively enhance and nurture the creative abilities of a team in relation to their ongoing responsibilities, fostering creativity within the team.

As a **Creative Director**, adopting an **inspiring and innovative tone**, could you suggest specific strategies or approaches that **I** can use to successfully improve and cultivate the **creative skills** of **my team members** while they continue to fulfill their regular job duties? This is particularly relevant given the goal of **fostering creativity within the team**.

As a **[profession]**, adopting a **[tone of voice]**, could you suggest specific strategies or approaches that **[I/Name/Role]** can use to successfully improve and cultivate the **[contextual challenge/opportunity]** of **[my/their] [team/group/department]** while they continue to fulfill their regular job duties? This is particularly relevant given the goal of **[desired outcome]**.

Example 1: As a Team Development Specialist, adopting a supportive and encouraging tone, could you suggest specific strategies or approaches that a research & development department head can use to successfully improve and cultivate the creative skills of their team while they continue to fulfill their research duties? This is particularly relevant given the goal of fostering creativity within the team.

Example 2: As a Leadership Development Consultant, adopting a motivational and energetic tone, could you suggest specific strategies or approaches that I can use to successfully improve and cultivate the creative skills of my insurance team members while they continue to fulfill their insurance-related duties? This is particularly relevant given the goal of fostering creativity within the insurance team.

PROMPT No 30

Meetings - Communication - Management

To gain insights on strategies to conduct effective and productive meetings when team members are considering significant decisions, enhancing team communication and management.

Given the challenge of **conducting effective meetings when team members are considering significant decisions such as resigning,** as an **HR Consultant** and in a **diplomatic and professional tone**, could you suggest strategies **I** can employ for **this purpose**?

Given the challenge of **[contextual challenge/opportunity],** as a **[profession]** and in a **[tone of voice],** could you suggest strategies **[I/Name/Role]** can employ for **[desired outcome]**?

Example 1: Given the challenge of conducting effective meetings when faculty members are considering significant decisions such as resigning, as a Leadership Development Facilitator and in a respectful and supportive tone, could you suggest strategies a department head can employ for this purpose?

Example 2: As a Change Management Consultant, in a clear and concise tone, could you suggest strategies I can employ to conduct effective and productive meetings with my IT team when they are considering a significant decision such as resigning from their positions? This advice is particularly relevant given the challenge of managing change in a volatile tech industry.

PROMPT No 31

Engagement - Discussion - Empowerment

To gain specific strategies and techniques for engaging in effective and fruitful discussions with a team, enabling them to independently determine where they should direct their energy and time.

As a **Leadership Development Consultant**, adopting a **collaborative and empowering tone**, could you suggest what strategies and techniques **I** can employ to engage in **effective and fruitful discussions** with **my team**, enabling them to **independently determine where they should direct their energy and time**?

As a **[profession]**, adopting a **[tone of voice]**, could you suggest what strategies and techniques **[I/Name/Role]** can employ to engage in **[desired outcome]** with **[my/their]** **[team/group/department]**, enabling them to **[contextual challenge/opportunity]**?

Example 1: As a Team Coach, adopting a supportive and respectful tone, could you suggest what strategies and techniques a project manager can employ to engage in effective and fruitful discussions with their project team, enabling them to independently determine where they should direct their energy?

Example 2: As a Business Consultant, adopting a professional and encouraging tone, could you suggest what strategies and techniques I can employ to engage in effective and fruitful discussions with my sales team, enabling them to independently determine where they should direct their time?

EXCITEMENT

PROMPT No 32

Persuasion - Investors - Excitement

To gain specific and effective tactics that can be utilized to create a sense of enthusiasm and interest among potential investors or stakeholders for a new business venture.

As a **Business Development Consultant**, adopting an **enthusiastic and persuasive tone**, could you provide me with specific and effective tactics that **I** can utilize to create a sense of **excitement and interest** among **potential investors or stakeholders** for a **new business venture**?

As a **[profession]**, adopting a **[tone of voice]**, could you provide me with specific and effective tactics that **[I/Name/Role]** can utilize to create a sense of **[desired outcome]** among **[contextual challenge/opportunity]** for a **[contextual challenge/opportunity]**?

Example 1: As a Venture Capitalist, adopting a confident and persuasive tone, could you provide me with specific and effective tactics that I can utilize to create a sense of excitement and interest among potential investors or stakeholders for a new tech startup?

Example 2: As a Startup Consultant, adopting an inspiring and enthusiastic tone, could you provide me with specific and effective tactics that I can utilize to create a sense of excitement and interest among potential investors or stakeholders for a new green energy venture?

PROMPT No 33

Energy - Enhancement - Transition

To gain specific strategies and techniques that can be implemented to successfully enhance and maintain high levels of team energy, specifically when faced with demanding projects or periods of transition.

As a **Team Development Specialist**, adopting an **encouraging and motivating tone**, could you suggest specific strategies and techniques that **I** can implement to successfully **enhance and maintain high levels of energy** within **my team**, particularly during **challenging projects or periods of transition**?

As a **[profession]**, adopting a **[tone of voice]**, could you suggest specific strategies and techniques that **[I/Name/Role]** can implement to successfully **[desired outcome]** within **[my/their] [team/group/department]**, particularly during **[contextual challenge/opportunity]**?

Example 1: As a Performance Coach, adopting a supportive and energetic tone, could you suggest specific strategies and techniques that an operations manager can implement to successfully enhance and maintain high levels of energy within their operations team, particularly during challenging projects?

Example 2: As a Leadership Development Consultant, adopting an inspiring and positive tone, could you suggest specific strategies and techniques that I can implement to successfully enhance and maintain high levels of energy within my sales team, particularly during challenging periods of market transition?

PROMPT No 34

Feedback - Recognition - Empowerment

To gain specific strategies and practices that can be implemented to effectively utilize feedback and recognition as tools for fostering a work environment that motivates and empowers team members to consistently perform at their best.

As a **Leadership Development Consultant**, adopting an **encouraging and supportive tone**, could you provide specific strategies and practices that **I** can implement to effectively utilize **feedback and recognition** as tools for fostering a work environment that **motivates and empowers my team members to consistently perform at their best**?

As a **[profession]**, adopting a **[tone of voice]**, could you provide specific strategies and practices that **[I/Name/Role]** can implement to effectively utilize **[contextual challenge/opportunity]** as tools for fostering a work environment that **[desired outcome]**?

Example 1: As a Team Coach, adopting a motivating and positive tone, could you provide specific strategies that a public relations manager can implement to effectively utilize feedback and recognition as tools for fostering a work environment that motivates and empowers their public relations team to consistently perform at their best?

Example 2: As an Executive Coach, adopting an inspiring and supportive tone, could you provide specific practices that I can implement to effectively utilize feedback and recognition as tools for fostering a work environment that motivates and empowers my quality assurance team to consistently perform at their best?

FEAR

PROMPT No 35

Tags
Empowerment - Ambition - Anxiety
Goal
To gain specific strategies for creating a nurturing and empowering atmosphere that motivates team members to wholeheartedly pursue ambitious objectives, even in the face of their own apprehensions and anxieties.
Prompt
As a **Leadership Development Consultant**, adopting a **supportive and encouraging tone**, could you provide specific strategies that **I** can implement to create a **nurturing and empowering atmosphere that motivates my team members to wholeheartedly pursue ambitious objectives,** even when they are faced with their own **apprehensions and anxieties**?
Formula
As a **[profession]**, adopting a **[tone of voice]**, could you provide specific strategies that **[I/Name/Role]** can implement to create a **[desired outcome]**, even when they are faced with their own **[contextual challenge/opportunity]**?
Examples
Example 1: As a Team Coach, adopting a motivating and positive tone, could you provide specific strategies that a sustainability manager can implement to create a nurturing and empowering atmosphere that motivates their sustainability team to wholeheartedly pursue ambitious objectives, even when they are faced with their own apprehensions and anxieties?
Example 2: As an Executive Coach, adopting an inspiring and supportive tone, could you provide specific strategies that I can implement to create a nurturing and empowering atmosphere that motivates my ethics and compliance team to wholeheartedly pursue ambitious objectives, even when they are faced with their own apprehensions and anxieties?

FEELINGS

PROMPT No 36

Tags
Empathy - Relationships - Improvement
Goal
To gain insights on specific actions and strategies that can be incorporated into daily life to actively improve the ability to empathize with and understand others on a deeper level.
Prompt

As a **Psychologist**, adopting a **compassionate and understanding tone**, could you provide me with specific actions and strategies that I can incorporate into my daily life to actively improve my ability to **empathize with and understand others on a deeper level**? This is particularly relevant given the goal of **enhancing interpersonal relationships and fostering a more empathetic environment**.

Formula

As a **[profession]**, adopting a **[tone of voice]**, could you provide me with specific actions and strategies that I can incorporate into my daily life to actively improve my ability to **[contextual challenge/opportunity]**? This is particularly relevant given the goal of **[desired outcome]**.

Examples

Example 1: As a Life Coach, adopting a supportive and encouraging tone, could you provide me with specific actions and strategies that I can incorporate into my daily life to actively improve my ability to empathize with and understand my executive team on a deeper level? This is particularly relevant given the goal of enhancing senior management relationships and fostering a more empathetic environment.

Example 2: As a Leadership Consultant, adopting a professional and understanding tone, could you provide me with specific actions and strategies that I can incorporate into my daily life to actively improve my ability to empathize with and understand my team members on a deeper level? This is particularly relevant given the goal of enhancing team dynamics and fostering a more empathetic work environment.

PROMPT No 37

Tags

Mental-Health - Support - Management

Goal

To gain specific strategies or techniques that can be utilized to efficiently manage a team member who is facing a notable decrease in mood as a result of their work or a particular project, fostering a supportive work environment and promoting mental well-being.

Prompt

As a **Mental Health Consultant**, adopting a **compassionate and understanding tone**, could you provide specific strategies or techniques that can be utilized to efficiently manage a **team member** who is facing a notable decrease in mood as a result of their work or a particular project? This is particularly relevant given the goal of fostering a supportive work environment and promoting mental well-being.

Formula

As a **[profession]**, adopting a **[tone of voice]**, could you provide specific strategies or techniques that can be utilized to efficiently manage a **[team/group/department member]** who is facing **[contextual challenge/opportunity]** as a result of their **[work/task/project]**? This is particularly relevant given the goal of **[desired outcome]**.

Examples

Example 1: As a Workplace Wellness Consultant, adopting a supportive and empathetic tone, could you provide specific strategies or techniques that can be utilized to efficiently manage a department member who is facing a notable decrease in mood as a result of their ongoing project? This is particularly relevant given the goal of fostering a supportive work environment and promoting mental well-being.

Example 2: As a Human Resources (HR) Manager, adopting a caring and understanding tone, could you provide specific strategies or techniques that can be utilized to efficiently manage a team member who is facing a notable decrease in mood as a result of their current workload? This is particularly relevant given the goal of fostering a supportive work environment and promoting mental well-being.

PROMPT No 38

Tags

Conversations - Understanding - Significance

Goal

To gain specific strategies or techniques to have meaningful conversations with team members that allow a deeper understanding of the importance and significance of their work, profession, or any other aspect of their lives, fostering a deeper understanding and connection within the team.

Prompt

As a **Leadership Coach**, adopting a **respectful and considerate tone**, could you provide specific strategies or techniques that **I** can employ to have meaningful conversations with **my team** members that allow **me** to delve deeper into the importance and significance of their work, profession, or any other aspect of their lives? This is particularly relevant given the goal of **fostering a deeper understanding and connection within the team**.

Formula

As a **[profession]**, adopting a **[tone of voice]**, could you provide specific strategies or techniques that **[I/Name/Role]** can employ to have meaningful conversations with **[my/their] [team/group/department]** members that allow **[me/them]** to delve deeper into the importance and significance of their work, profession, or any other aspect of their lives? This is particularly relevant given the goal of **[desired outcome]**.

Examples

Example 1: Adopting a patient and empathetic tone, as a Human Resources Consultant, could you provide specific strategies or techniques that a department head can employ to have meaningful conversations with their faculty members that allow them to delve deeper into the importance and significance of their work, profession, or any other aspect of their lives? This is particularly relevant given the goal of fostering a deeper understanding and connection within the faculty.

Example 2: As a Team Coach, adopting a supportive and open-minded tone, could you provide specific strategies or techniques that I can employ to have meaningful conversations with my project team members that allow me to delve deeper into the importance and significance of their work, profession, or any other aspect of their lives? This is particularly relevant given the goal of fostering a deeper understanding and connection within the project team.

FLOW

PROMPT No 39

Tags

Motivation - Productivity - Energy

Goal

To gain insights on specific steps and techniques that can be implemented to create a highly energized and motivated work environment, thereby increasing productivity and engagement among team members.

Prompt

As a **Motivational Speaker**, adopting an **inspiring and enthusiastic tone**, could you provide specific steps and techniques that **I** can take to create a **work environment** that is highly energized and motivated, thereby increasing **productivity and engagement** among **my team members**?

Formula

As a **[profession]**, adopting a **[tone of voice]**, could you provide specific steps and techniques that **[I/Name/Role]** can take to create a **[contextual challenge/opportunity]** that is highly energized and motivated, thereby increasing **[desired outcome]** among **[my/their] [team/group/department]**?

Examples

Example 1: As a Leadership Coach, adopting a positive and encouraging tone, could you provide specific steps and techniques that a department head can take to create a faculty environment that is highly energized and motivated, thereby increasing productivity and engagement among their faculty members?

Example 2: As a Team Development Consultant, adopting a proactive and solution-oriented tone, could you provide specific steps and techniques that I can take to create a project environment that is highly energized and motivated, thereby increasing productivity and engagement among my project team members?

PROMPT No 40

Tags

Empowerment - Focus - Productivity

Goal

To gain insights on how to effectively and consistently empower team members to reach their peak mental focus, productivity, and performance by implementing specific strategies and techniques.

Prompt

As a **Leadership Coach**, adopting a **motivational and supportive tone**, could you guide me on how to effectively and consistently empower **my team members** to reach their peak **mental focus, productivity, and performance** by implementing specific strategies and techniques?

Formula

As a **[profession]**, adopting a **[tone of voice]**, could you guide **[me/Name/Role]** on how to effectively and consistently empower **[my/their] [team/group/department]** to reach their peak **[contextual challenge/opportunity]** by implementing specific strategies and techniques?

Examples

Example 1: As a Team Development Consultant, adopting an encouraging and positive tone, could you guide a department head on how to effectively and consistently empower their faculty to reach their peak academic performance by implementing specific strategies and techniques?

Example 2: As a Performance Coach, adopting a motivational and supportive tone, could you guide me on how to effectively and consistently empower my sales team to reach their peak productivity and performance by implementing specific strategies and techniques?

FULFILLMENT

PROMPT No 41

Tags
Guidance - Objectives - Potential

Goal
To gain specific methods, steps, or tools that can be utilized to provide effective support and guidance to team members as they work towards accomplishing their personal professional objectives and reaching their full potential in their careers.

Prompt
As a **Career Coach**, adopting a **supportive and encouraging tone**, could you provide specific methods, steps, or tools that **I** can utilize to provide effective support and guidance to **my team members** as they work towards accomplishing their **personal professional objectives** and reaching their full potential in their careers?

Formula
As a **[profession]**, adopting a **[tone of voice]**, could you provide specific methods, steps, or tools that **[I/Name/Role]** can utilize to provide effective support and guidance to **[my/their] [team/group/department]** as they work towards accomplishing their **[contextual challenge/opportunity]** and reaching their full potential in their **[contextual challenge/opportunity]**?

Examples
Example 1: As a Leadership Development Consultant, adopting an empathetic and motivational tone, could you provide specific methods, steps, or tools that a department head can utilize to provide effective support and guidance to their faculty as they work towards accomplishing their academic objectives and reaching their full potential in their teaching careers? **Example 2:** As a Team Coach, adopting a positive and inspiring tone, could you provide specific methods, steps, or tools that I can utilize to provide effective support and guidance to my project team as they work towards accomplishing their project objectives and reaching their full potential in their project management careers?

GOALS

PROMPT No 42

Tags
Purpose - Professional - Personal

Goal

To gain insights on specific strategies and actions that can be implemented to effectively guide and support a team in discovering a sense of purpose both in their professional roles and personal lives.

As a **Life Coach**, adopting an **empathetic and supportive tone**, could you suggest specific strategies and actions **I** can implement to effectively guide and support **my team** in **discovering a sense of purpose both in their professional roles and personal lives**?

As a **[profession]**, adopting a **[tone of voice]**, could you suggest specific strategies and actions **[I/Name/Role]** can implement to effectively guide and support **[my/their]** **[team/group/department]** in **[desired outcome]**?

Example 1: As a Leadership Development Consultant, adopting a motivational and understanding tone, could you suggest specific strategies and actions a finance department head can implement to effectively guide and support their finance team in discovering a sense of purpose both in their professional roles and personal lives?

Example 2: As a Team Coach, adopting an encouraging and patient tone, could you suggest specific strategies and actions I can implement to effectively guide and support my government affairs team in discovering a sense of purpose both in their professional roles and personal lives?

PROMPT No 43

Synergy - Goal - Frameworks

To explore methods and frameworks to identify a pivotal goal that, when accomplished, would simplify or enable the achievement of other related objectives, providing a synergistic effect within an organization.

Act as a **Leadership Development Consultant** specializing in the **renewable energy industry**. Could you elucidate **the strategies, frameworks, or methods that can be employed to determine the goal that, once achieved, would simplify or enable other objectives within a team or organization**? This is central to **aligning efforts and maximizing efficiency in strategic planning**. Include uncommon advice and underrated resources in an all-encompassing and comprehensive manner, considering different organizational structures, cultures, and industries. Let's consider each facet of this topic. Write using an insightful tone and analytical writing style.

Act as a **[profession]** specializing in the **[industry of specialty]**. Could you elucidate **[contextual challenge/opportunity]**? This is central to **[desired outcome]**. Include uncommon advice and underrated resources in an all-encompassing and comprehensive manner, considering different organizational structures, cultures, and industries. Let's consider each facet of this topic. Write using a **[type]** tone and **[style]** writing style.

Example 1: Act as a Business Development Consultant specializing in the tech industry. Could you elucidate the process to identify the key goal that would catalyze other objectives within a startup? Share distinctive guidance and unexplored options. Let's dissect this carefully. Write using a motivational tone and creative writing style.

Example 2: Act as an Organizational Psychologist specializing in the education industry. Could you elucidate how to pinpoint the core objective that, once accomplished, would streamline other educational goals? Provide unique insights and overlooked opportunities. Let's think about this step by step. Write using a hopeful tone and descriptive writing style.

PROMPT No 44

Tags
Monitoring - Intervention - Accountability

Goal
To provide guidance on monitoring your team's progress toward annual goals and intervening appropriately when necessary. The focus is on understanding the ways to track progress, identify barriers, and provide constructive and polite intervention to ensure that the goals are met.

Prompt
Act as a **Performance Coach** specializing in the **food industry**. What are the **tools** I can employ to **continually** monitor my **team's** progress toward their **annual objectives**? How can I **identify potential obstacles**, and what are the **best practices** for **providing timely, constructive, and respectful interventions** to **ensure** they **stay on track** to **meet** their **goals**? What **strategies** can be **employed** to **create** a **supportive and accountable environment** without **micromanaging**? Let's **think this step by step**. Write using a **supportive** tone and **engaging** writing style.

Formula
Act as a **[profession]** specializing in the **[industry]**, what are the **[methods/tools/techniques]** I can employ to **[continually/consistently/regularly]** monitor my **[team's/department's/group's]** progress toward their **[annual/quarterly/monthly]** **[objectives/goals/targets]**? How can I **[identify/detect/recognize]** **[potential/possible/likely]** **[challenges/obstacles/barriers]**, and what are the **[best practices/guidelines/approaches]** for **[providing/offering]** **[timely/constructive/respectful]** **[interventions/support/assistance]** to **[ensure/guarantee/confirm]** they **[stay on track/remain aligned/keep focused]** to **[meet/achieve/accomplish]** their **[goals/targets/objectives]**? What **[strategies/tactics/methods]** can be **[employed/used/applied]** to **[create/build/develop]** a **[supportive/accountable/responsible]** **[environment/culture/atmosphere]** without *[micromanaging/overseeing excessively/over-controlling]*? Let's **[analyze/think about/consider]** this **[step by step/systematically]**. Write using a **[type]** tone and **[style]** writing style.

Examples
Example 1: Act as a Team Development Specialist specializing in the tech industry. What analytics and tools can I leverage to consistently oversee my software development team's progress toward their annual targets? How can I preemptively recognize obstacles and what mechanisms can I establish for polite, collaborative intervention to keep them aligned with their objectives? How can I foster a culture of accountability and encouragement without

crossing into micromanagement? Let's analyze this piece by piece. Write using an instructive tone and informative writing style.

Example 2: Act as an Executive Coach specializing in the retail industry. What tracking methodologies and communication strategies can I use to continually monitor my sales team's progress toward their yearly goals? How can I delicately intervene and provide support when challenges arise, ensuring the alignment of individual and organizational objectives? What are the best practices for balancing oversight and empowerment to promote team growth? Let's think about this step by step. Write using an empathetic tone and persuasive writing style.

PROMPT No 45

Tags

Professionalism - Improvement - Objectives

Goal

To facilitate the exploration and formulation of new professional objectives within a team, encouraging individual growth, alignment with organizational goals, and fostering a culture of continuous improvement and ambition. The ultimate aim is to empower team members to set challenging yet achievable targets that contribute to both personal development and overall team success.

Prompt

Act as a **Professional Development Coach** specializing in the **banking industry**. Could you guide me on how to **explore and articulate new professional objectives with my team that they could set for themselves**? This exploration is key to **stimulating growth, fostering alignment with company goals, and driving ambition within the team**. Please provide a comprehensive framework that includes individual **assessment techniques, goal-setting methodologies, collaboration strategies, and monitoring processes to ensure ongoing progress**. Let's approach this methodically. Write using an inspiring tone and instructive writing style.

Formula

Act as a **[profession]** specializing in the **[industry]**. Could you guide me on how to **[contextual challenge/opportunity]**? This exploration is key to **[desired outcome]**. Please provide a comprehensive framework that includes **[specific components or methods]**. Let's approach this methodically. Write using a **[type]** tone and **[style]** writing style.

Examples

Example 1: Act as a Team Development Specialist specializing in the technology industry. Could you guide me on how to help my software development team identify and set new professional objectives that align with our company's innovation goals? This exercise is vital to nurturing creativity, enhancing individual skills, and ensuring alignment with organizational vision. Please outline a structured approach that embraces personal assessment tools, SMART goal-setting, collaborative workshops, and ongoing mentorship programs. Let's dissect this carefully. Write using a motivating tone and engaging writing style.

Example 2: Act as a Leadership Coach specializing in the healthcare industry. Could you guide me on how to engage my medical staff in articulating and pursuing new professional objectives tailored to their unique roles and aspirations? This undertaking is essential for continuous professional development, alignment with patient-care excellence, and team cohesion. Please devise a multifaceted plan encompassing individual interviews, group discussions, career path mapping, and continuous feedback mechanisms. Let's analyze this piece by piece. Write using an empathetic tone and analytical writing style.

PROMPT No 46

Competency - Assessment - Talent-Assessment

To equip team leaders, managers, and HR professionals with a comprehensive toolkit for effectively assessing the fit between team members' skills and the organization's needs. This includes the implementation of competency models, talent assessments, and a deep dive into both soft and hard skills.

Act as a **Talent Management Specialist** specializing in **organizational alignment** for the **manufacturing industry**. Could you provide **a step-by-step guide to assess and determine the best fit between my team's skills and the organizational needs**? The ultimate goal is to **achieve higher team performance, job satisfaction, and long-term retention rates**. Your input should include **methods for evaluating both hard and soft skills**, a framework for matching these skills to company goals, and strategies for actionable follow-through. Explore unconventional solutions and alternative perspectives. Let's thoroughly explore each component for the most comprehensive understanding. Write using a **solution-oriented** tone and a **systematic** writing style.

Act as a **[profession]** specializing in **[topic/specialization]** for the **[industry]**. Could you provide **[contextual challenge/opportunity]?** The ultimate goal is to **[desired outcomes]**. Your input should include **[tools/techniques/considerations]**, a framework for matching these skills to company goals, and strategies for actionable follow-through. Explore unconventional solutions and alternative perspectives. Let's thoroughly explore each component for the most comprehensive understanding. Write using a **[type]** tone and **[style]** writing style.

Example 1: Act as a Team Dynamics Expert specializing in the tech industry. Could you lay out a structured approach for assessing the suitability of my software engineers' technical and interpersonal skills in relation to our project goals? The guide should include techniques for evaluating coding skills, problem-solving abilities, and team collaboration metrics. Additionally, it should offer ways to align these findings with our project objectives. Unearth hidden gems and non-traditional methods. Let's dig deep into each step of the process. Write using a practical tone and a data-driven writing style.

Example 2: Act as a Workforce Analyst specializing in healthcare. Could you delineate a comprehensive strategy for assessing the alignment between my nursing staff's clinical skills and the patient care objectives of our hospital? Your strategy should encompass methods for assessing both medical proficiency and bedside manner and offer actionable steps for addressing skill gaps. Discover rare insights and pioneering ideas. Let's break down each element for a complete picture. Write using an empathetic tone and an evidence-based writing style.

PROMPT No 47

Patterns - Management - Team-Development

To uncover and explore methodologies or strategies that can be utilized to identify recurring patterns or behaviors within a team throughout their career. Recognizing these patterns could lead to understanding underlying issues or habits and enable effective management, development, and growth.

Act as a **Team Development Specialist** specializing in the **e-commerce industry**. What are some ways in which **I can find out patterns that have been recurring for my team throughout their career**? Recognizing these patterns may assist in **identifying both opportunities and challenges that might impact their performance and personal development**. Present a detailed and broad-ranging response. Let's dissect this carefully. Write using an **analytical** tone and **informative** writing style.

Act as a **[profession]** in the **[industry]**. What are some ways in which **[contextual challenge/opportunity]**? Recognizing these patterns may assist in **[desired outcome]**. Present a detailed and broad-ranging response. Let's dissect this carefully. Write using an analytical tone and informative writing style.

Example 1: Act as an Organizational Psychologist specializing in the tech industry, could you elucidate the ways in which I can identify patterns recurring for my team throughout their career? Understanding these patterns might enable us to create targeted development programs, foster collaboration, and improve overall team efficiency. Share an exhaustive and in-depth response. Let's go through this systematically. Write using an insightful tone and engaging writing style.

Example 2: Act as an HR Consultant specializing in the banking industry, could you provide insight into the methodologies to observe and interpret patterns that have been persistent for my team throughout their career? Recognizing these patterns may lead to uncovering latent talents, mitigating potential risks, and tailoring personalized growth paths. Provide a meticulous and wide-ranging response. Let's consider each facet of this topic. Write using a professional tone and analytical writing style.

LEARNING

PROMPT No 48

Learning - Techniques - Comprehension

To explore diverse techniques and methodologies that a team can implement to learn and comprehend new topics or subjects efficiently. It emphasizes not just the acquisition of new knowledge but the understanding and application of that knowledge within a team setting.

Act as a **Professional Mentor** specializing in the **education sector**. What are some techniques **my team and I should consider to learn and understand any new topic**? This is crucial for **continuous growth, adapting to change, and enhancing our expertise in various domains**. Offer unconventional strategies and underused techniques. Let's dissect this carefully. Write using an **instructive** tone and **engaging** writing style.

Act as a **[profession]** specializing in the **[sector]**. What are some techniques **[contextual challenge/opportunity]**? This is crucial for **[desired outcome]**. Offer unconventional strategies and underused techniques. Let's dissect this carefully. Write using a **[type]** tone and **[style]** writing style.

Example 1: Act as a Talent Development Specialist specializing in the healthcare industry, what strategies should my team and I explore to effectively learn and comprehend new medical practices or techniques? The understanding of new methodologies is essential for innovation, patient care, and staying ahead in the rapidly evolving medical field. Share rare tips and lesser-known strategies. Let's consider each facet of this topic. Write using a confident tone and analytical writing style.

Example 2: Act as a Learning and Development Manager specializing in the IT industry, what approaches must my team and I adopt to learn and understand the latest technological advancements? Continual learning is key to innovation, problem-solving, and maintaining a competitive edge in our fast-paced industry. Ensuring that your response is thorough, precise, and of the highest quality possible. Let's think about this step by step. Write using an inspirational tone and creative writing style.

PROMPT No 49

Experiences - Beliefs - Self-Awareness

To help leaders effectively communicate to their teams the concept that individual experiences shape beliefs and assumptions. By achieving clarity on this topic, the team can better understand their behavior, make more informed decisions, and foster a culture of self-awareness and continuous improvement.

Act as a **Leadership Communication Expert** specializing in the **finance industry**. Could you provide **a comprehensive guide for explaining to my team how their personal experiences shape their beliefs and assumptions**? Include specific **strategies for presentation, the psychological underpinnings to consider, and a set of key talking points**. This is vital for **enhancing self-awareness and making better team decisions**. Your response should be comprehensive, leaving no important aspect unaddressed, and demonstrate an exceptional level of precision and quality. Let's dissect each element in a detailed manner. Write using an **empathetic** tone and an **instructive** writing style.

Act as a **[profession]** specializing in **[industry]**. Could you provide **[contextual challenge/opportunity]**? Include **[tools/strategies]**. This is vital for **[desired objective]**. Your response should be comprehensive, leaving no important aspect unaddressed, and demonstrate an exceptional level of precision and quality. Let's dissect each element in a detailed manner. Write using a **[type]** tone and **[style]** writing style.

Example 1: Act as an Organizational Development Consultant specializing in the healthcare sector. Could you offer a comprehensive guide to explain to my nursing staff how their experiences in different healthcare settings shape their beliefs and assumptions about patient care? The guide should cover presentation methods, relevant psychological theories, and talking points for discussion. This is essential for creating a more empathetic and effective patient care environment. Deliver an all-inclusive and extensive output. Let's break down each component for a better understanding. Write using a compassionate tone and a detailed, analytical writing style.

Example 2: Act as a Business Coach specializing in the food and beverage industry. Could you give a step-by-step approach for talking to my restaurant staff about how their experiences with customers and food preparation shape their beliefs and assumptions? Please include specific methods of communication, backed by psychological research, and key points to address during the conversation. This is key for improving both customer service and staff morale. Let's go through each part thoroughly. Write using an engaging tone and a practical, straightforward writing style.

PROMPT No 50

Tags

Blindspots - Leadership - Biases

Goal

help leaders in business settings identify and understand their blind spots. Blind spots are areas where a leader might have limitations or biases they are unaware of, which could affect their leadership effectiveness. Recognizing and addressing these blind spots can enhance a leader's ability to guide their team and make unbiased decisions.

Prompt

Act as a **Leadership Development Consultant** specializing in the **FinTech industry**. How can I **identify** my **blind spots** as a **leader**? What are the **tools** that can **help** me **uncover areas** where I might have **biases** that I'm **not aware of**? How can I **work** with my **team** to **gain insights** into these **hidden** areas, and what **steps** should I **take** to **address** them? What are some **examples** of **common leadership** blind spots, and how have **other** leaders successfully **overcome** them? Respond separately to each question. Suggest fresh approaches and inventive ideas. Let's take this one step at a time. Write using an **introspective** tone and **analytical** writing style.

Formula

Act as a **[profession]** specializing in the **[industry]**. How can I **[discover/identify/detect]** my **[blind spots/hidden biases/unknown limitations]** as a **[leader/guide/manager]**? What are the **[tools/techniques/strategies]** that can **[help/assist/guide]** me **[uncover/reveal/find]** **[areas/zones/aspects]** where I might have **[biases/limitations/restrictions]** that I'm **[not aware of/unconscious of/ignorant of]**? How can I **[work/collaborate/coordinate]** with my **[team/mentors/coaches]** to **[gain/obtain/acquire]** **[insights/knowledge/understanding]** into these **[hidden/obscured/unseen]** areas, and what **[steps/measures/actions]** should I **[take/implement/follow]** to **[address/resolve/rectify]** them? What are some **[examples/instances/cases]** of **[common/widespread/typical]** **[leadership/management/guidance]** blind spots, and how have **[other/successful/experienced]** leaders **[successfully/efficiently/effectively]** **[overcome/addressed/solved]** them? Respond separately to each question. Suggest fresh approaches and inventive ideas. Let's take this one step at a time. Write using a **[type]** tone and **[style]** writing style.

Example 1: Act as an Executive Coach specializing in the tech industry, how can I discover the unknown biases that might be affecting my leadership? What are the modern tools like 360-degree feedback or peer reviews that can assist me in identifying these areas? How can I engage with my team or professional network to gain insights and take corrective measures? What lessons can be learned from leaders who have addressed these issues successfully? Respond separately to each question. Discover rare insights and pioneering ideas. Let's unpack this topic. Write using a professional tone and informative writing style.

Example 2: Act as a Team Development Specialist specializing in the e-commerce industry, how can I detect areas where I might be inadvertently limiting my team due to my unrecognized biases? What practical strategies, such as self-reflection, mentorship, or seeking feedback, can help me uncover these aspects? How can I create an open and trusting environment that encourages candid feedback from my team, and what actionable steps can I follow to improve? What are some real-life examples of overcoming these leadership challenges? Respond separately to each question. Reveal lesser-known practices and innovative ideas. Let's dissect this carefully. Write using a confident tone and analytical writing style.

PROMPT No 51

Identification - Application - Performance

To gain specific strategies or methods that can be utilized to efficiently and accurately identify and access learning opportunities that are directly applicable to enhancing the performance and work of a team.

As a **Learning and Development Specialist**, adopting an **informative and supportive tone**, could you provide specific strategies or methods that **I** can utilize to efficiently and accurately identify and access learning opportunities that are directly applicable to enhancing the performance and work of **my sales team**?

As a **[profession]**, adopting a **[tone of voice]**, could you provide specific strategies or methods that **[I/Name/Role]** can utilize to efficiently and accurately identify and access learning opportunities that are directly applicable to **[desired outcome]** of **[my/their] [team/group/department]**?

Example 1: As a Corporate Trainer, adopting a clear and concise tone, could you provide specific strategies or methods that a department head can utilize to efficiently and accurately identify and access learning opportunities that are directly applicable to enhancing the performance and work of their IT team?

Example 2: As a Professional Development Coach, adopting an encouraging and motivational tone, could you provide specific strategies or methods that I can utilize to efficiently and accurately identify and access learning opportunities that are directly applicable to enhancing the performance and work of my marketing team?

PROMPT No 52

PositiveCulture -Productivity - KnowledgeTransfer

To provide organizational leaders with a well-rounded approach for transferring positive working experiences from a successful team to the broader company. This strategy aims to multiply the benefits of effective practices, thus improving the work culture, increasing productivity, and boosting overall job satisfaction.

Act as a **Corporate Culture Transformation Specialist** specializing in **positive work environments** for the **banking industry**. Could you provide a **detailed framework for how I can successfully transfer the positive working experiences within my team to the rest of the company**? This is key for **fostering a healthy organizational culture and replicating successful work habits on a larger scale**. Your guidance should include key aspects like knowledge dissemination, inter-departmental collaboration, and feedback loops. Examine overlooked possibilities and imaginative routes. Let's articulate each point for thorough understanding. Write using an **enthusiastic** tone and a **practical, actionable** writing style.

Act as a **[profession]** specializing in **[specialization/topic]** for the **[industry]**. Could you provide a **[specific challenge or opportunity]**? This is key for **[desired outcome]**. Your guidance should include **[tactics/methods/strategies]**. Examine overlooked possibilities and imaginative routes. Let's articulate each point for thorough understanding. Write using a **[type]** tone and **[style]** writing style.

Example 1: Act as a Leadership and Talent Development Consultant specializing in small to medium-sized enterprises. Could you elucidate a strategy for transferring the positive work experiences within my product design team to other departments within the company? This is essential for scaling the values and practices that have made this team highly productive. Your advice should delve into methods for capturing best practices, employee testimonials, and setting up internal mentorship programs. Propose rejuvenated methodologies and ingenious plans. Let's deconstruct the problem methodically.
Write using an uplifting tone and a hands-on writing style.

Example 2: Act as an Organizational Behavior Analyst specializing in the technology sector. Could you guide me on how to expand the successful agile practices from my engineering team to our marketing and customer service departments? This is pivotal for implementing a cohesive and efficient work structure across the company. Your guide should discuss cultural considerations, inter-departmental training programs, and mechanisms for ongoing evaluation. Uncover scarce wisdom and trailblazing concepts. Let's parse the topic into manageable chunks. Write using an analytical tone and an evidence-based writing style.

PROMPT No 53

ContinuousLearning - Self-awareness - LessonLearned

To foster a culture of continuous learning by creating an environment where team members can openly discuss and extract the most significant lessons from both recent successes and failures. The goal is to help the team understand the factors that contributed to the outcome, reinforce positive behaviors, and identify areas for improvement.

Act as a **Business Learning and Development Expert** specializing in **reflective practices** for the **investment banking industry**. Could you offer a **comprehensive guide** on how **to effectively lead a team discussion centered around the most significant lesson learned from a recent success or failure**? I am interested in **methods that encourage self-awareness, critical thinking, and collective wisdom**. Please include **segments on setting the agenda, question prompts, and follow-up activities to ensure ongoing learning**. Impart unconventional wisdom and under-the-radar tools. Let's go through this systematically. Write using an encouraging tone and a future-focused writing style.

Act as a **[profession]** specializing in **[specialization/expertise]** for the **[industry]**. Could you offer a **[type of resource/tool]** on how to **[specific task]**? I am interested in **[particular methods/techniques]**. Please include **[distinct elements of the discussion/stages/activities]**. Impart unconventional wisdom and under-the-radar tools. Let's go through this systematically. Write using a **[type]** tone and **[style]** writing style.

Example 1: Act as a Leadership Coach specializing in team motivation. Could you provide a structured plan on how to discuss and learn from the key lessons of a recently completed project? I want to focus on elevating team morale while we dissect what went well and what didn't. Please include mood-setting activities, key questions for reflection, and steps for acknowledging and celebrating the team's effort. Share distinctive guidance and unexplored options. Let's dissect this carefully. Write using an inspiring tone and a motivational writing style.

Example 2: Act as a Cognitive Psychologist specializing in decision-making processes. Could you offer a psychological framework for discussing the biggest takeaways from a recent success or failure in our team's work? I am keen on understanding the cognitive biases that may have affected our decisions and outcomes. Include exercises for identifying these biases, strategies for avoiding them in the future, and follow-up activities for continuous improvement. Provide unusual recommendations and overlooked tools. Let's consider each facet of this topic. Write using an analytical tone and a research-based writing style.

PROMPT No 54

Authenticity - Communication   - Introspection

To foster authentic communication and self-awareness by guiding you in discussing what you've learned from a recent challenge. The objective is to ensure that your reflections are not only insightful but also sincere, which can help to cultivate trust and openness within your team while promoting personal growth.

Act as a **Communication Coach** with expertise in **leadership transparency**. Could you provide a **detailed guide** on how to **genuinely discuss what I have learned from**

facing a recent challenge? I'm specifically looking for a **structured approach that includes a set of key questions I should consider, conversational techniques to maintain authenticity, and psychological tips to encourage introspection**. Segment this guide into clear steps and ensure all advice is actionable. Let's think about this step by step. Write using an **honest** tone and a **straightforward** writing style.

Act as a **[profession]** with expertise in **[specialized area]**. Could you provide a **[type of guide/resource]** on how to **[specific challenge/opportunity]?** I'm specifically looking for **[particular elements/techniques]**. Segment this guide into clear steps and ensure all advice is actionable. Let's think about this step by step. Write using a **[specified tone]** and **[writing style].**

Example 1: Act as a Leadership Consultant specialized in emotional intelligence. Could you outline a guide on how to authentically share what I've learned from a recent setback with my team? I'd like to focus on leveraging emotional intelligence to ensure that my reflections resonate with my team. Include a set of reflection questions, strategies to detect and manage emotions, and a sample script for initiating the discussion. Break down the guide into pre-conversation preparation, the conversation itself, and post-conversation reflections. Let's go through this systematically. Write using a compassionate tone and an engaging writing style.

Example 2: Act as an Organizational Behavior Expert focused on team dynamics. Could you develop a guide for discussing my learnings from a recent challenge in a way that promotes collective learning within my team? I'm particularly interested in techniques that not only allow me to share but also encourage my team to reflect on similar experiences they may have had. Provide activities that can be done as a team, question prompts for group discussions, and steps for documenting the shared learning. Let's dissect this carefully. Write using a collaborative tone and an instructional writing style.

PROMPT No 55

Leadership - Risk-Management - Reflection

To help leaders facilitate discussions or reflections where team members can identify and articulate instances where they successfully navigated challenges or took calculated risks that led to positive outcomes. This serves multiple purposes: validating the team's skills and decision-making, boosting morale, and distilling insights that can be applied in future challenges.

Act as a **Leadership and Risk Management Expert** for the **publishing industry**. Could you provide a **comprehensive guide** on how to **guide my team in articulating a situation where they successfully managed a challenge, took a risk, and it paid off**? I'd like to explore **a range of strategies that facilitate this conversation, including question prompts, possible activities, and ways to record and disseminate these success stories for future learning within the team and organization**. Develop a comprehensive and penetrating insight. Let's think about this step by step. Write using an **informative** tone and **factual** writing style.

Act as a **[profession]** specializing in the **[industry]**. Could you provide a **[comprehensive guide/detailed framework]** on how to **[specific challenge or objective]**? I would like to explore **[sub-goals/specific techniques]**. Develop a comprehensive and penetrating insight. Let's think about this step by step. Write using an informative tone and factual writing style.

Examples

Example 1: Act as a Career Development Coach specializing in storytelling techniques. Could you provide a structured approach on how to guide my team to articulate examples where they overcame professional obstacles and succeeded? I want to help them master the art of storytelling to effectively share these experiences within and outside our team. Please include storytelling frameworks, question prompts for team discussions, and templates for recording these stories. Establish an all-embracing and methodical evaluation. Let's analyze this piece by piece. Write using a diplomatic tone and tactful writing style.

Example 2: Act as an Organizational Psychologist specializing in reflective practice. Could you offer a comprehensive methodology for encouraging my team to discuss past challenges they've successfully overcome? I'm particularly interested in group activities that facilitate open dialogue and mutual learning. Please include guidelines for creating a psychologically safe space, group activities that encourage sharing, and strategies to compile these learnings into a team "Success Story" handbook. Craft a rigorous and exhaustive investigation. Let's dissect this carefully. Write using a friendly tone and approachable writing style.

LISTENING

PROMPT No 56

Tags

Problem-Solving - Bottleneck-Identification - Innovation

Goal

To enhance the understanding and skill set of identifying bottlenecks, challenges, or areas where a team might be stuck within a project or problem, and exploring strategies, methods, or tools to effectively overcome these challenges.

Prompt

Act as a **Problem-Solving Specialist** specializing in the **technology industry**. Could you provide **an in-depth analysis of the techniques, strategies, and tools that I can employ to identify where my team is most stuck in a project or problem**? This is critical for **timely intervention and to facilitate the progress of ongoing projects**. Include both conventional wisdom and innovative approaches, considering various team dynamics, project complexity, and industries. Let's **dissect this carefully**. Write using an **instructive** tone and **analytical** writing style.

Formula

Act as a **[profession]** specializing in the **[industry]**. Could you provide **[contextual challenge/opportunity]**? This is critical for **[desired outcome]**. Include both conventional wisdom and innovative approaches, considering various team dynamics, project complexity, and industries. Let's **[approach]**. Write using a **[type]** tone and **[style]** writing style.

Examples

Example 1: Act as a Project Management Consultant specializing in the construction industry. Could you provide a meticulous analysis of the methods and tools to pinpoint where my construction team might be facing delays or challenges in a project? This is crucial for optimizing workflow and ensuring timely completion. Include actionable strategies and novel insights. Let's analyze this piece by piece. Write using a professional tone and constructive writing style.

Example 2: Act as a Team Efficiency Expert specializing in the marketing industry. Could you provide a detailed exploration of the techniques to determine where my marketing team might be struggling or stuck in a campaign development process? This is vital for improving productivity and achieving the campaign's goals. Share distinctive guidance and unexplored options, considering various team structures and marketing strategies. Let's think about this step by step. Write using a confident tone and creative writing style.

MINDSET

PROMPT No 57

Tags
Work-Environment - Empowerment - Assessment

Goal
To equip team with comprehensive strategies for assessing the impact of the current work environment on their team's performance and well-being. This evaluation aims to identify factors that either empower or limit the team, enabling leaders to make data-driven adjustments to the work environment.

Prompt
Act as an **Organizational Psychologist** specializing in **Workplace Environment and Team Dynamics** for **biotechnology industry**.   Could you provide an **exhaustive guide** on **how to assess whether the current work environment is either limiting or empowering my team**? I'm particularly interested in questionnaires, observational techniques, and real-time analytics that can give me a holistic view. Please divide the guide into manageable sections and include illustrative examples and case studies to clarify key points. Investigate unexpected avenues and creative pathways. Let's scrutinize this topic incrementally. Write using an analytical tone and systematic writing style.

Formula
Act as a **[profession]** specializing in **[expertise/topic]** for the **[industry]**. Could you provide an **[all-encompassing guide/manual/resource]** on **[contextual challenge/opportunity]**? I am particularly interested in **[types of methods/approaches/tools]**. Please divide the **[guide/resource]** into **[stages/sections/steps]**. Investigate unexpected avenues and creative pathways. Let's scrutinize this topic incrementally. Write using a **[type]** tone and **[style]** writing style.

Examples
Example 1: Act as a Workplace Wellness Consultant with a focus on Team Productivity. Could you deliver a structured guide on assessing the current work environment's impact on my team's productivity and well-being? I am keen on integrating employee surveys and environmental scans into the assessment. Break down the process into actionable steps, and provide statistical data and research to back up your suggestions. Suggest fresh approaches and inventive strategies. Let's examine each dimension meticulously. Write using a data-driven tone and an academic writing style.   **Example 2:** Act as a Leadership Coach specializing in Team Engagement. Could you offer a detailed roadmap on evaluating how the current work environment influences my team's

engagement levels? I am interested in employing focus groups and one-on-one interviews for a qualitative analysis. Please partition the guide into thematic areas and include testimonials and anecdotal evidence to illustrate the importance of an empowering environment. Discover rare insights and pioneering ideas. Let's deconstruct this subject stepwise. Write using an empathetic tone and a narrative writing style.

PROMPT No 58

Team-Dynamics - Awareness - Questioning

To create a well-rounded resource that equips leaders and managers with pointed questions aimed at facilitating team members' awareness of their operating mindsets. The objective is to encourage self-reflection, spark open discussions, and inspire shifts towards more constructive mindsets that enhance productivity and team dynamics.

Act as a **Business Psychologist** specializing in **Cognitive Dynamics in a Team Setting** for the Energy industry. Could you provide an **exhaustive list of questions** designed to **prompt my team members to become more aware of their operating mindsets**? I am especially interested in **questions that elicit insights into default thinking patterns, emotional triggers, and interpersonal dynamics**. Also, include guidance on when and how to ask these questions for maximal impact. Please divide the material into **three parts: initial assessment, ongoing development, and intervention scenarios**. Identify latent opportunities and avant-garde approaches. Let's consider each facet of this topic. Write using a supportive and insightful tone.

Act as a **[profession]** specializing in **[topic/expertise]** for the **[industry]**. Could you provide a **[comprehensive guide/list/resource]** designed to **[contextual challenge/opportunity]**? I am especially interested in **[areas of focus/types of methods]**. Please divide the **[guide/list/resource]** into **[sections/stages/steps]**. Identify latent opportunities and avant-garde approaches. Let's consider each facet of this topic. Write using a **[type]** tone and **[style]** writing style.

Example 1: Act as an Organizational Development Consultant with a focus on Emotional Intelligence. Could you supply an all-inclusive list of questions that will encourage my team to examine their operating mindset? I am interested in incorporating emotional intelligence metrics into these questions. Sort the list into categories like self-awareness, social awareness, and decision-making and include tips on when these questions would be most effective in team meetings. Unveil under-the-radar tactics and groundbreaking schemes. Let's take this one step at a time. Write using a nurturing tone and a comprehensive style.

Example 2: Act as a Leadership Coach specializing in High-Performance Teams. Could you offer a guide that contains questions intended to awaken my team members to their prevailing mindsets? I am keen on questions that challenge limiting beliefs and provoke a growth mindset. Organize the material into contexts such as project kickoffs, mid-project reviews, and post-project debriefs, providing timing strategies for each. Elaborate on fresh perspectives and audacious strategies. Let's unpack this topic.Write using an empowering tone and a forward-thinking style.

PROMPT No 59

Tags

Possibilities - Reflection - Engagement

Goal

To equip team leaders, managers, and executives with an exhaustive framework for fostering a culture of reflection and possibility within their teams. This framework aims to help team members explore the full range of opportunities and potentials in their current roles, thereby boosting engagement, satisfaction, and productivity.

Prompt

Act as an **Organizational Development Consultant** specializing in **employee engagement** for the **SaaS industry**. Could you guide me through **a comprehensive method to help my team reflect on what's possible in their current roles**? Please offer specific methods and **conversation guides** to foster progress. Additionally, identify any **overlooked opportunities** that might be encountered. Explore unconventional solutions and alternative perspectives. Let's tackle this step by step. Write using an **in-depth** tone and a **structured** writing style.

Formula

Act as a **[profession]** specializing in **[topic/specialization]** for the **[industry]**. Could you guide me through **[contextual challenge/opportunity]**? Please offer specific methods and **[specific tools/exercises/conversation guides/tracking metrics]** to foster progress. Additionally, identify any **[overlooked opportunities/potential obstacles]**. Explore unconventional solutions and alternative perspectives. Let's tackle this step by step. Write using a **[type]** tone and **[style]** writing style.

Examples

Example 1: Act as a Talent Development Manager specializing in career progression for the retail industry. Could you provide a systematic approach to help my sales team contemplate the opportunities available to them within their current positions? I'd like to focus on skill-building and upward mobility. Suggest interactive workshops, mentorship programs, and key performance indicators for gauging success. Also, let's address potential distractions and how to overcome them. Let's explore this rigorously. Write using a detailed tone and a logical writing style.

Example 2: Act as a Team Culture Strategist specializing in motivation and team dynamics for the hospitality sector. Can you help me design a framework for my customer service team to reflect on the possibilities for growth and job satisfaction in their current roles? I'm particularly interested in incorporating mindfulness and positive psychology. Provide step-by-step activities, reflection templates, and recommended books or resources. Also, indicate potential pitfalls like burnout and how to mitigate them. Let's go through this carefully. Write using a supportive tone and a practical writing style.

PROMPT No 60

Tags

Empathy - Career - Feedback

Goal

To obtain a comprehensive, methodical approach for leadership development in the technology sector, focusing on understanding team members' career aspirations. It seeks actionable strategies in conversation techniques, feedback mechanisms, assessment tools, and ongoing support, all delivered in an empathetic and engaging tone.

Act as a **Leadership Development Specialist** specializing in the **technology industry**. Could you guide me on how I can **effectively discover what my team members are actively pursuing in their professional careers**? Understanding **their professional goals, interests, and aspirations** is vital for **my team synergy, motivation, and alignment with our company's mission and vision**. Please provide a detailed and methodical approach, including **conversation techniques, feedback strategies, assessment tools, and a plan for ongoing support**. Let's dissect this carefully. Write using an **empathetic** tone and **engaging** writing style.

Act as a **[profession]** specializing in the **[industry]**. Could you guide me on how I can **[contextual challenge/opportunity]**? Understanding **[desired outcome]** is vital for **[specific team or organizational goals]**. Please provide a detailed and methodical approach, including **[specific techniques or tools]**. Let's dissect this carefully. Write using a **[type]** tone and **[style]** writing style.

Example 1: Act as a Team Building Coach specializing in the healthcare industry. Could you advise me on how I can uncover what my medical team members are striving for in their individual careers? Realizing their unique ambitions and aligning them with our healthcare goals can lead to a more harmonious and committed team environment. Please detail the steps, including one-on-one meetings, goal-setting workshops, personalized development plans, and continuous feedback mechanisms. Let's analyze this piece by piece. Write using an inspirational tone and constructive writing style.

Example 2: Act as a Career Development Mentor specializing in the education sector. Could you enlighten me on how I can learn about my faculty members' professional pursuits and academic aspirations? This information is essential for fostering personal growth and aligning their ambitions with our institution's educational objectives. Please outline a comprehensive approach, including surveys, mentoring programs, regular check-ins, and personalized training paths. Let's take this one step at a time. Write using a supportive tone and informative writing style.

PROMPT No 61

Readiness - Team-Dynamics - Project-Management

To equip business leaders with insights and strategies to accurately gauge their team's readiness to take specific actions for progressing on projects. Understanding team readiness is crucial for optimizing resource allocation, setting realistic timelines, and ensuring the quality of project outcomes.

Act as a **Project Management Consultant** with a specialization in **team dynamics** for the **tech industry**, could you guide me through **assessing what actions my team is ready to take to move their projects forward**? Please include **frameworks for readiness assessment and techniques to elicit honest and constructive feedback**. Make sure to cover how **to evaluate both individual and collective readiness levels**.

Unfold alternative perspectives and pioneering approaches to sustain this practice. Let's dissect this in a structured manner. Write using an **informative** tone and a **factual** writing style.

Act as a **[profession]** with a specialization in **[area of expertise]** for the **[industry]**, could you guide me through **[specific challenge/opportunity]**? Please include **[methods/techniques]**. Make sure to cover how **[key areas/topics]**. Unfold alternative perspectives and pioneering approaches to sustain this practice. Let's dissect this in a structured manner. Write using a **[type]** tone and **[style]** writing style.

Example 1: Act as a Change Management Specialist with a specialization in corporate transformations, could you guide me through evaluating my team's readiness to adopt a new software suite? Please include risk assessments, behavioral cues, and appropriate timelines. Make sure to cover how to integrate readiness metrics into change management dashboards. Unfold alternative perspectives and pioneering approaches to sustain this practice. Let's dissect this in a structured manner. Write using a consultative tone and a comprehensive writing style.

Example 2: Act as a Leadership Coach with a specialization in motivation and commitment in the manufacturing industry, could you guide me through determining my team's willingness to adopt a continuous improvement program? Please include diagnostic questionnaires and one-on-one interview techniques. Make sure to cover how to address any apprehensions or resistance. Unfold alternative perspectives and pioneering approaches to sustain this practice. Let's dissect this in a structured manner. Write using an empathetic tone and a relatable writing style.

OPTIONS

PROMPT No 62

Opportunities - Development - Learning

To equip leaders with a robust framework for identifying opportunities within problems that can serve as catalysts for their team's professional development, thereby fostering a culture of continuous learning and adaptability.

Act as a **Professional Development Coach** specializing in the **SaaS industry**. Could you **elucidate** the **strategies** for **identifying opportunities** within **problems** that **my** team could **leverage** for **further professional development**? Include **analytical tools, problem-solving methodologies, and team workshops that can be utilized**.

Let's systematically explore each facet. Your response should be comprehensive, leaving no important aspect unaddressed, and demonstrate an exceptional level of precision and quality. Write using an analytical tone and a prescriptive writing style.

Act as a **[profession]** specializing in the **[industry]**. Could you **[elucidate/explain/guide]** the **[strategies/methodologies/approaches]** for **[identifying/spotting/uncovering] [opportunities/chances/potentials]** within

[problems/challenges/issues] that **[my/our/the]** team could **[leverage/utilize/exploit]** for **[further/additional/ongoing]** **[professional/career]** development? Include **[analytical tools/problem-solving methodologies/team workshops]**. Let's systematically explore each facet. Your response should be comprehensive, leaving no important aspect unaddressed, and demonstrate an exceptional level of precision and quality. Write using a **[type]** tone and **[style]** writing style.

Example 1: Act as a Career Development Advisor specializing in the healthcare industry. Could you explain the methodologies for spotting chances within challenges that my nursing team could utilize for ongoing career development? Include SWOT analysis, root cause analysis, and peer mentoring programs. Let's piece-by-piece analyze this matter. Write using a supportive tone and an instructive writing style. Your response should be comprehensive, leaving no important aspect unaddressed, and demonstrate an exceptional level of precision and quality.

Example 2: Act as a Leadership Consultant specializing in the retail sector. Could you guide me through the approaches for uncovering potentials within issues that my sales team could exploit for additional professional growth? Include brainstorming sessions, after-action reviews, and skills gap analysis. Let's carefully evaluate each segment. Write using an inspiring tone and a motivational writing style. Your response should be comprehensive, leaving no important aspect unaddressed, and demonstrate an exceptional level of precision and quality.

PROMPT No 63

Stability - Individual-Preferences - Human-Resources

To gain insights on strategies to effectively initiate a discussion with team members regarding their individual preferences for either stability or challenge in their work environment, fostering a work environment that meets individual needs and enhances team satisfaction and performance.

Given the goal of **understanding individual preferences for stability or challenge in the work environment**, as a **Human Resources Consultant** and in a **diplomatic and professional tone**, could you suggest strategies **I** can employ to effectively initiate a discussion with **my team members**?

Given the goal of **[contextual challenge/opportunity]**, as a **[profession]** and in a **[tone of voice]**, could you suggest strategies **[I/Name/Role]** can employ to effectively initiate a discussion with **[my/their]** **[team/group/department]**?

Example 1: Given the goal of understanding individual preferences for stability or challenge in a dynamic startup environment, as a Business Coach and in an open-minded and respectful tone, could you suggest strategies a startup founder can employ to effectively initiate a discussion with their team members?

Example 2: As an Employee Engagement Manager, in a considerate and inclusive tone, could you suggest strategies I can employ to effectively initiate a discussion with my sales team regarding their individual preferences for either stability or challenge in their work environment? This advice is particularly relevant given the goal of improving team satisfaction and performance.

PROMPT No 64

Tags

Decision-Making - Transparency - Leadership

Goal

To develop a set of strategies, techniques, and frameworks for improving decision-making skills within a team. This involves understanding the dynamics of decision-making, factors influencing decisions, potential biases, the role of data, and collaborative decision-making processes. The focus is on practical solutions, case examples, training, and mentoring practices to build a cohesive and efficient decision-making process within the team.

Prompt

Act as a **Decision-making Coach** specializing in the **Cybersecurity industry**. Decision-making is a **crucial** aspect of **professional** life that **influences** the **outcomes** of **projects** and the overall success of an organization. What are some **proven strategies** that can be used to **enhance** the decision-making skills of a **team**? How can **understanding cognitive biases** improve the **quality** of decisions? Additionally, how can **leadership** cultivate a culture of **transparent** decision-making? Share **examples** demonstrating the **successful** implementation of these strategies within the **Cybersecurity industry**. Respond separately to each question. Deliver all-inclusive and extensive responses. Let's take this one step at a time. Write using a formal tone and concise writing style.

Formula

Act as a **[profession]** specializing in the **[industry]**. Decision-making is a **[critical/essential/vital]** aspect of **[professional/organizational/team]** life that **[influences/impacts/affects]** the **[outcomes/results/success]** of **[projects/endeavors/initiatives]**. What are some **[proven/effective/practical]** **[strategies/techniques/models]** that can be used to **[enhance/improve/build]** the decision-making skills of a **[team/group/organization]**? How can **[list factors such as understanding cognitive biases, using collaborative tools]** improve the **[quality/efficiency/effectiveness]** of decisions? Additionally, how can **[leadership/management/team members]** cultivate a culture of **[transparent/inclusive/responsible]** decision-making? Share **[examples/case studies/scenarios]** demonstrating the **[successful/efficient/proven]** implementation of these strategies within the **[industry]**. Respond separately to each question. Deliver all-inclusive and extensive responses. Let's take this one step at a time. Write using a **[type]** tone and **[style]** writing style.

Examples

Example 1: Act as a Leadership Trainer specializing in the tech industry, decision-making is a vital aspect of project management that affects the success of software development. What are some practical techniques, such as SWOT analysis, risk assessment, and Agile methodologies, that can be employed to improve the decision-making skills of a tech team? How can collaboration platforms, data-driven insights, and a focus on ethical considerations contribute to more informed decisions? Additionally, how can tech leaders foster an environment where every team member feels empowered to contribute to decision-making? Share case studies from leading tech companies that have excelled in decision-making processes. Respond separately to each question. Include uncommon advice and underrated views. Let's dissect this carefully. Write using an innovative tone and analytical writing style.

Example 2: Act as a Performance Coach specializing in the banking industry, decision-making is an essential part of financial planning that influences the outcomes of investment strategies. What are some effective strategies, such as financial modeling, risk analysis, compliance checks, and team brainstorming, that banking professionals can use to enhance decision-making? How can understanding market trends, regulatory requirements, and ethical obligations lead to sound financial decisions? Additionally, how can bank executives create a culture that encourages transparent and collective decision-making? Share real-life examples from renowned banking institutions that have successfully navigated complex decision-making scenarios. Respond separately to each question. Provide unique insights and overlooked opportunities. Let's dissect this carefully. Write using a professional tone and detailed writing style.

PERFORMANCE

PROMPT No 65

Tags
Self-Awareness - Performance - Coaching
Goal
To gain insights on effective techniques to increase a team's self-awareness regarding their optimal performance, fostering a high-performing and self-aware work environment.
Prompt
In the context of **enhancing self-awareness for optimal performance**, as a **Performance Coach** and in an **encouraging and supportive tone**, could you outline some effective techniques **I** can adopt with **my team**?
Formula
In the context of **[contextual challenge/opportunity]**, as a **[profession]** and in a **[tone of voice]**, could you outline some effective techniques **[I/Name/Role]** can adopt with **[my/their] [team/group/department]**?
Examples
Example 1: In the context of enhancing self-awareness for optimal performance in a high-stress environment, as a Leadership Development Facilitator and in a patient and considerate tone, could you outline some effective techniques a department head can adopt with their team? **Example 2:** As a Talent Development Specialist, in an empowering and optimistic tone, could you outline some effective techniques I can adopt with my customer service team to increase their self-awareness regarding their optimal performance? This advice is particularly relevant in the context of improving customer satisfaction.

PROMPT No 66

Tags
Communication - Trust-Building - Inclusivity
Goal
To outline and explore various strategies, behaviors, practices, and attitudes that a leader or manager can adopt to foster and improve their relationship with their team. This includes the importance of effective communication, empathy, trust-building, providing constructive

feedback, recognizing achievements, and promoting an inclusive culture. It aims to provide insights, guidelines, and actionable advice for leaders striving for a more harmonious and productive team environment.

Act as a **Team Relationship Expert** specializing in the **consumer goods manufacturing industry**. Building and maintaining a **positive** relationship with your team is **foundational** to **achieving success and fostering a healthy work environment**. What are some **key behaviors** that **leaders** must **adopt** to **enhance** their relationships with **team members**? How does **effective communication** contribute to a **stronger** team **connection**? Share **practical steps** illustrating how these **steps** can be implemented within the **consumer goods manufacturing industry**. Respond separately to each question. Deliver an all-inclusive and extensive commentary. Write using a **friendly** tone and **approachable** writing style.

Act as a **[profession]** specializing in the **[industry]**. Building and maintaining a **[positive/healthy/strong]** relationship with your team is **[foundational/critical/essential]** to **[achieving/attaining/reaching]** **[success/growth/harmony]**. What are some **[key/essential/important]** **[strategies/behaviors/techniques]** that **[leaders/managers/supervisors]** must **[adopt/implement/employ]** to **[enhance/improve/strengthen]** their relationships with **[team members/staff/colleagues]**? How does **[select a factor such as effective communication, empathy, regular feedback]** contribute to a **[stronger/more cohesive/better]** team **[connection/bond/relationship]**? Share **[practical steps/examples/scenarios]** illustrating how these **[principles/guidelines/concepts]** can be **[implemented/applied/put into practice]** within the **[industry]**. Respond separately to each question. Deliver an all-inclusive and extensive commentary. Write using a **[type]** tone and **[style]** writing style.

Example 1: Act as a Leadership Development Consultant specializing in the tech industry, building and maintaining a strong relationship with your team is critical to achieving innovation and success. What are some vital techniques, such as regular one-on-ones, open-door policies, team-building activities, and active listening, that tech leaders can implement to improve their connection with team members? How do empathy, clear communication, constructive feedback, and recognition of achievements contribute to a more cohesive tech team? Share practical examples from leading tech companies demonstrating the successful adoption of these relationship-building practices. Respond separately to each question. Deliver an all-inclusive and extensive commentary. Write using an analytical tone and systematic writing style.

Example 2: Act as an Executive Coach specializing in the logistics industry, fostering a positive relationship with your team is foundational to maintaining efficiency and productivity. What are some essential strategies, such as transparent communication, trust-building exercises, conflict resolution techniques, and regular team meetings, that logistics leaders must adopt to strengthen their relationship with staff? How does inclusivity, valuing diversity, and acknowledging individual contributions enhance team morale and cooperation? Share real-life scenarios from various logistics companies that have benefited from focusing on these relationship-improvement methodologies. Respond separately to each question. Deliver an all-inclusive and extensive commentary. Write using a motivational tone and inspiring writing style.

Achievement - Self-Reflection - Marketing

To guide you in initiating conversations with your team members regarding their proudest achievements, and how this self-reflection can lead to understanding their driving forces, aligning with organizational values, and guiding future behavior and professional growth.

Act as a **Career Development Specialist** specializing in the **marketing industry**. Could you help me understand **how to have meaningful conversations with my team members about what they are most proud of in their careers**? I would like to understand **how this self-reflection can influence their motivation, align them with our company's values, and guide their future decisions and behaviors**. Please provide step-by-step guidance, conversation frameworks, insightful questions, and methods for integrating these insights into our daily workflow and long-term development plans. Suggest fresh approaches and inventive strategies. Let's analyze this piece by piece. Write using an **encouraging** tone and **interactive** writing style.

Act as a **[profession]** specializing in the **[industry]**. Could you help me understand **[contextual challenge/opportunity]**? I would like to understand **[desired outcome]**. Please provide step-by-step guidance, conversation frameworks, insightful questions, and methods for integrating these insights into our daily workflow and long-term development plans. Suggest fresh approaches and inventive strategies. Let's analyze this piece by piece. Write using a **[type]** tone and **[style]** writing style.

Example 1: Act as an Employee Engagement Consultant specializing in the finance industry. Could you help me discover how to talk with my team about their most rewarding experiences in their careers? I want to comprehend how these reflections can enhance their commitment, align them with our organizational goals, and influence their future choices and actions. Please provide conversation starters, motivational techniques, personalized approaches, and ways to embed these reflections into our performance reviews and team meetings. Discover rare insights and pioneering ideas. Let's dissect this carefully. Write using a motivating tone and thoughtful writing style.

Example 2: Act as a Leadership Coach specializing in the non-profit sector. Could you guide me on how to discuss with my team members their most gratifying accomplishments? I am interested in how this self-awareness can bolster their passion, help them resonate with our mission, and direct their ongoing development and teamwork. Please share dialogue techniques, reflective exercises, case studies, and strategies for applying these insights in volunteer coordination and project planning. Render an in-depth and wide-spectrum response. Let's explore this step by step. Write using an inspirational tone and engaging writing style.

PREFERENCES

Trust-building - Mentorship - OpenDialogue

To equip business leaders and managers with the strategies, tools, and psychological insights needed to create a safe space for open, honest dialogue with their team members about the aspects they find both inspiring and uninspiring about the company.

Act as a **Communication and Trust-building Expert** specializing in **coaching and mentoring** for the **tech industry**. Could you guide me through **techniques for discussing with my team what they find the most inspiring and uninspiring about the company**? I aim to do this in a way that encourages openness without inducing feelings of threat or judgment. Provide a systematic approach, including how to set the environment, types of questions to ask, and strategies for ensuring confidentiality and psychological safety. Let's unpack this carefully. Share tailored guidance and personalized insights. Write using a **compassionate** tone and a **detailed** writing style.

Act as a **[profession]** specializing in **[topic]** for the **[industry]**. Could you guide me through **[contextual challenge/opportunity]**? I aim to facilitate this dialogue in a manner that encourages openness without causing fear or apprehension. Provide a systematic approach, including setting the environment, formulating questions, and ensuring confidentiality and psychological safety. Share tailored guidance and personalized insights. Let's unpack this carefully. Write using a **[Tone]** tone and a **[Style]** writing style.

Example 1: Act as a Leadership Coach specializing in emotional intelligence and trust-building for the finance industry. Could you help me develop techniques for discussing with my team members what they find the most inspiring and uninspiring about our corporate culture? I aim to foster a non-threatening and open environment for this dialogue. Please provide step-by-step guidance on how to set up these conversations, what types of questions to ask, and how to handle confidentiality and emotional safety. Moreover, offer strategies for incorporating this feedback into our talent development programs. Let's explore this carefully. Write using an empathetic tone and a supportive writing style.

Example 2: Act as an Organizational Psychologist specializing in team dynamics and feedback mechanisms for the healthcare industry. Could you assist me in framing conversations with my healthcare team about what they find both uplifting and discouraging about our organization? I aim to establish a psychologically safe space for these talks. Kindly outline how to prepare, what questions to pose, and how to reassure participants about confidentiality and their well-being. Also, offer insight into how this feedback can be channeled into operational and leadership improvements. Let's scrutinize this methodically. Write using a respectful tone and an informative writing style.

PRIORITIES

PROMPT No 69

Goal-setting - Finance - Strategic Planning

To guide business leaders in strategically prioritizing their goals in a manner that aligns with the overall objectives of the organization, individual career aspirations, and team development needs. Prioritizing goals effectively is essential for maintaining focus, maximizing resources, and achieving sustainable results.

Act as a **Business Strategy Consultant** with a specialization in **goal-setting** for the **finance industry**, could you guide me through **the process of prioritizing my goals in relation to the others I have been working on**? Please include **frameworks like the Eisenhower Matrix, or Objectives and Key Results (OKRs) for setting priorities, and techniques for regular reassessment**. Make sure to cover how **to balance short-term objectives against long-term strategic aims**. Unfold alternative perspectives and pioneering approaches to sustain this practice. Let's dissect this in a structured manner. Write using an **insightful** tone and an **analytical** writing style.

Act as a **[profession]** with a specialization in **[area of expertise]** for the **[industry]**, could you guide me through **[specific challenge/opportunity]**? Please include **[methods/techniques]**. Make sure to cover how **[key areas/topics]**. Unfold alternative perspectives and pioneering approaches to sustain this practice. Let's dissect this in a structured manner. Write using a **[type]** tone and **[style]** writing style.

Example 1: Act as a Life Coach with a specialization in personal development for the education industry, could you guide me through prioritizing my teaching goals for the academic year? Please include various methods like the MoSCoW method or SMART goals to arrange them in order of importance. Make sure to cover how to align these priorities with curriculum requirements and personal growth. Unfold alternative perspectives and pioneering approaches to sustain this practice. Let's dissect this in a structured manner. Write using a motivational tone and an inspiring writing style.

Example 2: Act as an Organizational Psychologist with a specialization in workforce performance for the retail industry, could you guide me through setting priorities for my team's sales targets? Please include performance metrics and indicators to track success, as well as suggestions for routine check-ins with team members. Make sure to cover how to align these priorities with the company's quarterly financial goals. Unfold alternative perspectives and pioneering approaches to sustain this practice. Let's dissect this in a structured manner. Write using a practical tone and a detailed writing style.

PROGRESS

PROMPT No 70

Well-being - Mental-Health - Productivity

To develop a deep, actionable understanding of how each team member's strengths manifest in their work and responsibilities, thereby enabling the leader to foster a workplace that amplifies these strengths for enhanced productivity and employee engagement.

As a **team leader** specializing in **Human Resources** within the **finance industry**, provide an exhaustive and meticulous examination, incorporating innovative insights and inventive strategies, for consciously identifying observable indicators or patterns that signify how each team member's strengths manifest in **tasks such as data analysis, customer**

interactions, and project management. Further, share detailed guidance on how to disseminate these insights to secure buy-in from stakeholders.

As a [profession] specializing in [area of expertise/focus] within the [industry], provide an exhaustive and meticulous examination, incorporating innovative insights and inventive strategies, for consciously identifying observable indicators or patterns that signify how each team member's strengths manifest in [specific tasks or responsibilities]. Further, share detailed guidance on how to disseminate these insights to secure buy-in from stakeholders.

Example 1: As a Marketing Manager specializing in digital advertising within the consumer goods industry, provide an exhaustive and meticulous examination, incorporating innovative insights and inventive strategies, for consciously identifying observable indicators or patterns that signify how each team member's strengths manifest in activities like campaign planning, SEO optimization, and consumer research. Further, share detailed guidance on how to disseminate these insights to secure buy-in from stakeholders.

Example 2: As a Principal Investigator specializing in biomedical research within the healthcare sector, provide an exhaustive and meticulous examination, incorporating innovative insights and inventive strategies, for consciously identifying observable indicators or patterns that signify how each research team member's strengths manifest in tasks such as data collection, analysis, and academic writing. Further, share detailed guidance on how to disseminate these insights to secure buy-in from stakeholders.

PROMPT No 71

Planning - Project-Management - Collaboration

To guide leaders, managers, or team leads in understanding, developing, and implementing an effective and actionable plan for their team's success in projects.

Act as an expert **Project Manager** with a focus on **team dynamics and success planning** for the **technology industry**. Could you outline a detailed roadmap for **setting up a team for success in their projects**? Include the **identification of goals, alignment with organizational objectives, collaboration strategies, roles and responsibilities, monitoring progress, and continuous improvement mechanisms**. Provide insights tailored to my role as **project leader**. Let's break down the process in a **systematic and sequential manner**. Write with **clarity**, providing **practical examples, and addressing potential pitfalls**.

Act as an expert **[profession]** with a focus on **[specific area of expertise]** for the **[industry]. Could you outline a detailed roadmap for [specific task or challenge]**? Include the **[list of detailed considerations]**. Provide insights tailored to my role as **[position/role]**. Let's break down the process in a **[structured manner]**. Write with **[specific writing tone and style]**, providing **[additional content details]**.

Example 1: Act as an expert Agile Coach with a focus on cross-functional team collaboration. Could you outline a detailed roadmap for setting up an Agile team for success in software development projects? Include the definition of sprint goals, collaboration with stakeholders, team roles, daily stand-up meetings, retrospectives, and Kanban boards. Provide insights tailored to startups, different development methodologies, remote vs. in-house teams, and common bottlenecks. Let's dissect the process in a logical and iterative manner. Write with an engaging tone, providing real-world examples and addressing the misconceptions.

Example 2: Act as an expert Operations Manager with a focus on manufacturing efficiency. Could you outline a detailed roadmap for optimizing a manufacturing team's performance in a series of production projects? Include goal-setting, alignment with organizational KPIs, coordination between different departments, quality control, progress tracking, and Lean methodologies. Provide insights tailored to various manufacturing industries, production scales, team dynamics, and compliance considerations. Let's analyze the process in a hierarchical and sequential fashion. Write with a professional tone, providing case studies and addressing potential regulatory challenges.

PROMPT No 72

Tags

Motivation - OrganizationalBehavior - Stagnation

Goal

To empower leaders with actionable strategies, psychological insights, and communication methods for effectively motivating their teams, especially when facing a standstill or a decline in performance. These guidelines should assist in reinvigorating team morale, refocusing efforts, and generating a newfound sense of progress.

Prompt

Act as a **Motivational Strategist** specializing in **organizational behavior** for the **natural resources industry**. Could you provide a comprehensive guide on **how I can better motivate my team when we are encountering stagnation or lack of progress in our work**? This is vital for **re-energizing the team, improving productivity, and aligning with our overall company goals**. Your guidance should touch on **communication strategies, psychological tactics, and actionable steps**, while also highlighting what to avoid. Explore unconventional solutions and alternative perspectives. Let's take this one step at a time. Write using an encouraging tone and a pragmatic writing style.

Formula

Act as a **[profession]** specializing in **[topic/specialization]** for the **[industry]**. Could you offer a detailed guide on **[contextual challenge/opportunity]**? This is vital for **[desired outcome]**. Your guidance should touch on **[detailed parameters, including x, y, z]**, while also noting what to avoid. Explore unconventional solutions and alternative perspectives. Let's take this one step at a time. Write using a **[type]** tone and **[style]** writing style.

Examples

Example 1: Act as a Team Engagement Consultant specializing in the technology sector. Could you lay out a set of actionable methods that I can implement to motivate my software development team during periods where we are not making noticeable progress? This is crucial for maintaining enthusiasm, boosting efficiency, and facilitating innovation. Your suggestions should cover both intrinsic and extrinsic motivational factors, and provide a timeline for implementing these strategies. Suggest fresh approaches and inventive strategies. Let's think about this step by step. Write using an optimistic tone and an evidence-based writing style.

Example 2: Act as an Organizational Psychologist specializing in retail. Could you provide a thorough breakdown of strategies for uplifting my customer service team when they are facing a slump in performance metrics? This is critical for reviving the spirit of the team, improving customer satisfaction, and meeting sales targets. Your recommendations should encompass empathy-based communication, goal re-evaluation, and the role of managerial support. Discover rare insights and pioneering ideas. Let's go through this systematically. Write using a compassionate tone and a solutions-oriented writing style.

PURPOSE

PROMPT No 73

Tags
Emotional - Articulation - Morale

Goal
To acquire a comprehensive, actionable guide on methods for exploring the emotional connection a team has with their purpose and assisting them in articulating it, with the aim of enhancing team morale, individual well-being, and organizational alignment.

Prompt
As an **Emotional Intelligence Coach** in the **automotive industry**, could you provide an exhaustive guide outlining the methods **I** can employ to explore the emotional connection **my team** has with their **purpose** and assist them in describing it? Please include both **reflective exercises and group discussion techniques**. Break down your advice into specific sections, reinforcing each with **quantifiable metrics and scholarly literature**. Explore unconventional approaches and diverse viewpoints. Let's dissect this carefully. Write using a **balanced** tone and a **nuanced** writing style.

Formula
As a **[profession]** in the **[industry]**, could you provide an exhaustive guide outlining the methods **[I/Name/Role]** can employ to explore the emotional connection **[my/our/their]** **[team/group/department]** has with their **[purpose/goals/values]** and assist them in describing it? Please include both **[reflective exercises/group discussion techniques]**. Break down your advice into specific sections, reinforcing each with **[quantifiable metrics/scholarly literature]**. Explore unconventional approaches and diverse viewpoints. Let's dissect this carefully. Write using a **[type]** tone and **[style]** writing style.

Examples

Example 1: As a Team Dynamics Specialist in the technology sector, could you provide an exhaustive guide outlining the methods a project manager can employ to explore the emotional connection their software development team has with their purpose and assist them in articulating it? Please include both individual reflection prompts and team brainstorming sessions. Divide your insights into separate modules, each validated by empirical findings and authoritative sources. Investigate unexpected avenues and creative pathways. Let's examine each dimension meticulously. Write using a focused tone and a concise writing style.

Example 2: As a Leadership Development Consultant in the retail industry, could you provide an exhaustive guide outlining the methods I can employ to explore the emotional connection my customer service team has with their purpose and assist them in describing it? Please include both guided meditations and facilitated group dialogues. Structure your guidance into individual components, each backed by statistical analysis and peer-reviewed studies. Unearth hidden gems and non-traditional methods. Let's tackle this in a phased manner. Write using an analytical tone and a structured writing style.

PROMPT No 74

Tags
Commitment - Dialogue - Performance

Goal
To guide business leaders in facilitating effective conversations with their teams about their willingness to take action and do what it takes to succeed. The objective is to assess team members' commitment levels, identify potential barriers, and create an actionable plan for heightened team performance and success.

Prompt
Act as a **Leadership Development Coach** with a specialization in **team dynamics and commitment** for the **technology industry**. Could you guide me through **the process of engaging my team in a dialogue about their willingness to take action and do what it takes to succeed?** Please include **methods for initiating the conversation, questions to gauge willingness, and techniques for fostering a safe environment for open dialogue**. Make sure to cover how **to create a feedback loop and an actionable plan based on the conversation**. Discover rare insights and pioneering ideas to help motivate the team further. Let's dissect this in a structured manner. Write using an **informative** tone and a **factual** writing style.

Formula
Act as a **[profession]** with a specialization in **[area of expertise]** for the **[industry]**. Could you guide me through **[specific challenge/opportunity]?** Please include **[methods/techniques]**. Make sure to cover how **[key areas/topics]**. Discover rare insights and pioneering ideas. Let's dissect this in a structured manner. Write using a **[type]** tone and **[style]** writing style.

Examples

Example 1: Act as an Organizational Psychologist with a specialization in employee engagement for the healthcare industry, could you guide me through evaluating my team's willingness to adapt to new technologies? Please include icebreakers to initiate conversation, questions that help gauge openness, and techniques for reducing resistance to change. Make sure to cover how to develop training programs based on the assessments. Unearth hidden gems and non-traditional methods to make technology adoption smoother. Let's dissect this in a structured manner. Write using an analytical tone and systematic writing style.

Example 2: Act as a Business Consultant with a specialization in organizational behavior for the manufacturing industry, could you guide me through assessing my team's readiness to take on additional responsibilities? Please include workshops to kick off the conversation, questions to evaluate readiness, and group exercises for skill-building. Make sure to cover how to realign task delegation based on the discussion. Navigate through unexplored realms and revolutionary paradigms to facilitate team growth. Let's dissect this in a structured manner. Write using a friendly tone and approachable writing style.

PROMPT No 75

Tags
Engagement - Purpose - Satisfaction

Goal
To gain specific steps or techniques that can be implemented as a leader to improve the capacity to have meaningful conversations with team members about their work's purpose and satisfaction, thereby fostering deeper engagement.

Prompt
As a **Leadership Coach**, adopting a **supportive and engaging tone**, could you provide specific steps or techniques that **I** can implement as a leader to improve my capacity to have meaningful conversations with **my team members** about their **work's purpose and satisfaction**? This is particularly relevant given the goal of **fostering deeper engagement within the team**.

Formula
As a **[profession]**, adopting a **[tone of voice]**, could you provide specific steps or techniques that **[I/Name/Role]** can implement as a leader to improve my capacity to have meaningful conversations with **[my/their] [team/group/department]** about their **[contextual challenge/opportunity]**? This is particularly relevant given the goal of **[desired outcome]**.

Examples
Example 1: As a Team Development Consultant, adopting a collaborative and empathetic tone, could you provide specific steps or techniques that a department head can implement as a leader to improve their capacity to have meaningful conversations with their faculty about their academic purpose and satisfaction? This is particularly relevant given the goal of fostering deeper engagement within the faculty.
Example 2: As a Corporate Trainer, adopting a motivational and inspiring tone, could you provide specific steps or techniques that I can implement as a project manager to improve my capacity to have meaningful conversations with my project team about their project's purpose and satisfaction? This is particularly relevant given the goal of fostering deeper engagement within the project team.

PROMPT No 76

Tags
Resilience - Problem-Solving - Support

Goal
To gain specific actions, techniques, or tools to improve the capacity to effectively support and lead a team in difficult situations, fostering resilience and effective problem-solving within the team.

Prompt
As a **Leadership Development Consultant**, adopting a **solution-oriented and supportive tone**, could you provide specific actions, techniques, or tools that **I** can utilize to improve **my** capacity to effectively support and lead **my team** in **difficult situations**? This is particularly relevant given the goal of fostering resilience and effective problem-solving within the team.

Formula
As a **[profession]**, adopting a **[tone of voice]**, could you provide specific actions, techniques, or tools that **[I/Name/Role]** can utilize to improve **[my/their]** capacity to effectively support and lead **[my/their]** **[team/group/department]** in **[contextual challenge/opportunity]**? This is particularly relevant given the goal of **[desired outcome]**.

Examples
Example 1: Adopting a solution-oriented and supportive tone, as a Team Coach, could you provide specific actions, techniques, or tools that a project manager can utilize to improve their capacity to effectively support and lead their project team in high-stress situations? This is particularly relevant given the goal of fostering resilience and effective problem-solving within the project team. **Example 2:** As a Management Consultant, adopting a strategic and empathetic tone, could you provide specific actions, techniques, or tools that I can utilize to improve my capacity to effectively support and lead my sales team in competitive market situations? This is particularly relevant given the goal of fostering resilience and effective problem-solving within the sales team.

PROMPT No 77

Tags
Perception - Alignment - Duties

Goal
To guide team leaders and managers in assisting their team members to comprehend the way they perceive and frame their duties. This understanding will enhance self-awareness, enable better communication and collaboration within the team, and align individual responsibilities with team goals and organizational values.

Prompt
Act as a **Team Dynamics Specialist** specializing in the **automotive industry**. Could you elucidate **the strategies and techniques that I can employ to help my team realize how they frame their duties in relation to their work and interactions with the**

rest of their team? This understanding is vital for **fostering collaboration, aligning individual tasks with team objectives, and promoting a harmonious working environment**. Please provide a thorough and actionable guide that covers various approaches, psychological insights, communication methods, and **team-building activities**. Let's dissect this carefully. Write using an **instructive** tone and **engaging** writing style.

Act as a **[profession]** specializing in the **[industry]**. Could you elucidate **[contextual challenge/opportunity]?** This understanding is vital for **[desired outcome]**. Please provide a thorough and actionable guide that covers various approaches, psychological insights, communication methods, and **[specific factors or elements]**. Let's dissect this carefully. Write using a **[type]** tone and **[style]** writing style.

Example 1: Act as a Communication Strategist specializing in the technology industry. Could you delineate the ways I can assist my software development team to recognize how they perceive and frame their roles and responsibilities in relation to the project and each other? This insight is crucial for enhancing teamwork, aligning coding standards, and facilitating effective knowledge sharing. Please present an exhaustive blueprint including emotional intelligence tools, Agile methodologies, regular feedback loops, and facilitated group discussions. Let's analyze this piece by piece. Write using a professional tone and analytical writing style.

Example 2: Act as an Organizational Psychologist specializing in the hospitality industry. Could you guide me through the process of helping my customer service team understand how they view and frame their individual duties with respect to customer interactions and team coordination? This awareness is essential for improving customer satisfaction, building a cohesive team, and reinforcing brand values. Please create an all-inclusive playbook embracing empathy exercises, role-playing scenarios, shared success stories, and continuous performance evaluations. Let's approach this systematically. Write using an empathetic tone and constructive writing style.

PROMPT No 78

Empowerment - Leadership - Self-awareness

To enable individuals, especially leaders and managers, to identify areas in their work and relationships where they may unconsciously relinquish control or influence. This insight is crucial for self-awareness, empowerment, and effective leadership, ensuring that they maintain the appropriate level of authority and confidence in their interactions and decisions.

Act as an **Executive Coach** specializing in the **finance industry**. Could you guide me through **a reflective analysis to discover the areas of my work and responsibilities where I tend to give away my power in work relationships**? Recognizing these areas is essential for **strengthening my leadership, enhancing collaboration, and maintaining the integrity of my role**. Please provide a detailed roadmap that includes **self-assessment tools, strategies for observation, guidance on seeking feedback, and methods to reclaim and assert my influence**. Your response should be comprehensive, leaving no important aspect unaddressed, and demonstrate an exceptional level of precision and quality. Let's dissect this carefully. Write using an **insightful** tone and **engaging** writing style.

Act as a **[profession]** specializing in the **[industry]**. Could you guide me through **[contextual challenge/opportunity]**? Recognizing these areas is essential for **[desired outcome]**. Please provide a detailed roadmap that includes **[specific components or methods]**. Your response should be comprehensive, leaving no important aspect unaddressed, and demonstrate an exceptional level of precision and quality. Let's dissect this carefully. Write using a **[type]** tone and **[style]** writing style.

Example 1: Act as a Leadership Mentor specializing in the technology industry. Could you direct me to uncover the aspects of my project management where I tend to cede control in team interactions? Understanding these facets is key to boosting my leadership effectiveness, ensuring project alignment, and building a resilient team dynamic. Please craft an exhaustive guide that considers personality assessments, mentorship, peer review, and leadership training modules. Offer an in-depth and exhaustive response. Let's analyze this piece by piece. Write using a confident tone and analytical writing style.

Example 2: Act as a Relationship Management Consultant specializing in the healthcare industry. Could you help me identify the parts of my supervisory role where I may inadvertently relinquish authority in interactions with my nursing staff? Gaining this insight is fundamental for fortifying my management capabilities, fostering trust, and harmonizing the hierarchical structure. Please design an all-inclusive strategy that integrates emotional intelligence evaluation, one-on-one coaching, 360-degree feedback, and assertiveness workshops. Share a full and in-depth response. Let's approach this methodically. Write using an empathetic tone and constructive writing style.

PROMPT No 79

Assessment - Leadership - Analytical

To provide leaders with a robust framework for self-assessment that identifies their unique contributions to team dynamics and performance. The objective is to enhance self-awareness, optimize individual strengths, and ultimately improve team outcomes.

Act as a **Leadership Assessment Specialist** specializing in the **tech industry**. How can I **rigorously** assess the **unique** ways in which I **contribute** to my **team's success**? Include **methodologies, key performance indicators, and real-world examples**. Let's sequentially unravel this issue. Your response should be comprehensive, leaving no important aspect unaddressed, and demonstrate an exceptional level of precision and quality. Write using an **analytical** tone and a **data-driven** writing style.

Act as a **[profession]** specializing in the **[industry]**. How can I **[rigorously/thoroughly/comprehensively]** assess the **[unique/specific/individual]** ways in which I **[contribute/add value/participate]** to my **[team's/group's/organization's]** **[success/performance/effectiveness]**? Include **[methodologies/techniques/tools]**, **[key performance indicators/metrics/measures]**, and **[real-world examples/case studies/practical illustrations]**. Let's sequentially unravel this issue. Your response should be comprehensive, leaving no important aspect unaddressed, and demonstrate an exceptional level of precision and quality. Write using a **[type]** tone and **[style]** writing style.

Example 1: Act as a Team Dynamics Analyst specializing in the healthcare industry. How can I comprehensively assess the specific ways in which I add value to my medical team? Include psychometric tests, patient satisfaction metrics, and case studies from successful healthcare teams. Let's examine each dimension meticulously. Write using a reflective tone and an evidence-based writing style. Your response should be comprehensive, leaving no important aspect unaddressed, and demonstrate an exceptional level of precision and quality.

Example 2: Act as a Leadership Coach specializing in the finance sector. How can I rigorously assess the individual ways in which I participate in my team's effectiveness? Include SWOT analysis, financial KPIs, and real-world examples from high-performing finance teams. Let's deconstruct this subject stepwise. Write using a strategic tone and a solution-oriented writing style. Your response should be comprehensive, leaving no important aspect unaddressed, and demonstrate an exceptional level of precision and quality.

PROMPT No 80

Collaboration - Accountability - Consultative

To equip leaders with a comprehensive framework for effectively involving external stakeholders in various project contexts, thereby enhancing collaboration, accountability, and project success.

Act as a **Leadership Consultant** specializing in the **technology sector**. Could you outline a **structured approach** for involving **external stakeholders** in a **software development project**? What are the **key considerations, best practices, and potential pitfalls**? Provide **actionable steps and innovative solutions**, each supported by **evidence or case studies**. Let's **methodically dissect each component**. Write using a **consultative** tone and an **advisory** writing style.

Act as a **[profession]** specializing in the **[industry]**. Could you outline a **[structured approach/methodology]** for involving **[external stakeholders/partners/clients]** in a **[specific project/context]**? What are the **[key considerations/critical factors/essential elements]**, **[best practices/recommended approaches]**, and **[potential pitfalls/common mistakes]**? Provide **[actionable steps/concrete measures]** and **[innovative solutions/creative ideas]**, each supported by **[evidence/case studies/references]**. Let's **[methodically dissect each component/examine each dimension meticulously]**. Write using a **[type]** tone and **[style]** writing style.

Example 1: Act as a Project Management Expert specializing in the healthcare industry. Could you delineate a comprehensive strategy for involving external stakeholders in a hospital expansion project? What are the vital considerations, proven methods, and common errors to avoid? Offer step-by-step guidance and groundbreaking solutions, each substantiated by industry research. Let's systematically explore each facet. Write using a quality-focused tone and meticulous writing style.

Example 2: Act as a Business Strategy Consultant specializing in the retail sector. Could you provide a detailed framework for involving suppliers and partners in a new product launch? What are the essential elements, best practices, and pitfalls to be wary of? Present actionable tactics and avant-garde strategies, each backed by successful case studies. Let's carefully evaluate each segment. Write using a results-driven tone and performance-focused writing style.

PROMPT No 81

Recognition - Interpersonal - Reflective

To enable managers, team leaders, and even team members themselves to systematically evaluate the unique strengths and qualities each individual contributes to their interactions with clients or colleagues. By doing so, we aim to foster a culture of recognition, promote skills development, and improve team cohesion.

Act as an **Organizational Psychologist** with a specialization in **interpersonal relationships** for the **non-profit sector**. Could you guide me through **methods to reflect on the unique strengths and qualities my team members bring to their relationships with clients and colleagues**? Please include **assessment frameworks, reflective questions, and qualitative data gathering techniques**. Make sure to cover how **to encourage team members to recognize and leverage their own and others' strengths in these relationships**. Explore unconventional solutions and alternative perspectives to nurture these skills. Let's dissect this in a structured manner. Write using an **insightful** tone and a **how-to** guide style.

Act as a **[profession]** with a specialization in **[area of expertise]** for the **[industry]**. Could you guide me through **[specific challenge/opportunity]**? Please include **[methods/techniques]**. Make sure to cover how **[key areas/topics]**. Explore unconventional solutions and alternative perspectives to nurture these skills. Let's dissect this in a structured manner. Write using a **[type]** tone and **[style]** writing style.

Example 1: Act as a Talent Development Specialist with a specialization in employee engagement for the retail industry. Could you guide me through a structured approach to identify and celebrate the strengths my sales team members use when interacting with customers? Please include metrics for evaluating customer satisfaction, methodologies for recognizing individual contributions, and team meetings structures to highlight these successes. Make sure to cover how to effectively communicate this information back to the team. Delve into uncharted territories and groundbreaking concepts for rewards and recognition. Let's dissect this in a structured manner. Write using an inspiring tone and a persuasive writing style.

Example 2: Act as an Executive Coach with a specialization in leadership development for the consulting industry. Could you guide me through techniques to measure and improve the relational skills that my team members exhibit during client consultations? Please include KPIs related to client relationships, emotional intelligence assessments, and feedback loops. Make sure to cover how to motivate team members to refine their client interaction skills. Discover rare insights and pioneering ideas to reinforce the importance of these skills. Let's dissect this in a structured manner. Write using an authoritative tone and a technical writing style.

PROMPT No 82

Tags

Leadership - Effectiveness - Performance

Goal

To acquire a comprehensive, actionable guide on methods for determining the support or resources that the leaders of a company need to enhance their work performance, with the aim of improving leadership effectiveness, team productivity, and overall organizational success.

Prompt

As an **Executive Coach** in the **telecommunications industry**, could you provide an exhaustive guide outlining the methods **I** can employ to determine the support or resources the leaders of **my company** need to enhance their **work performance**? Please include diagnostic **tools like 360-degree feedback and resource allocation strategies**. Segment the guide into **distinct categories**, and substantiate each with empirical data. Explore unconventional approaches and diverse viewpoints. Let's dissect this carefully. Write using an **analytical** tone and a **structured** writing style.

Formula

As a **[profession]** in the **[industry]**, could you provide an exhaustive guide outlining the methods **[I/Name/Role]** can employ to determine the support or resources the leaders of **[my/our/their]** **[company/organization]** need to enhance their **[work performance/specific area of** performance]? Please include **[diagnostic tools like X/resource allocation strategies like Y]**. Segment the guide into **[distinct categories]**, and substantiate each with **[empirical data/scholarly references]**. Explore unconventional approaches and diverse viewpoints. Let's dissect this carefully. Write using a **[type]** tone and **[style]** writing style.

Examples

Example 1: As a Leadership Development Consultant in the healthcare industry, could you provide an exhaustive guide outlining the methods a hospital administrator can employ to determine the support or resources the department heads need to enhance their patient care performance? Please include both performance metrics and budget reallocation strategies. Divide the guide into key areas, and validate each with clinical studies and peer-reviewed articles. Investigate unexpected avenues and creative pathways. Let's examine each dimension meticulously. Write using a focused tone and a concise writing style.

Example 2: As an Organizational Development Specialist in the retail sector, could you provide an exhaustive guide outlining the methods I can employ to determine the support or resources the store managers need to enhance their sales performance? Please include both customer satisfaction surveys and staff training programs. Break the guide into actionable steps, and corroborate each with industry benchmarks and case studies. Unearth hidden gems and non-traditional methods. Let's tackle this in a phased manner. Write using a balanced tone and a nuanced writing style.

PROMPT No 83

Tags
Self-assessment - Motivation - Development

Goal
To meticulously identify and develop or modify personal attributes in a manner that significantly augments one's ability to achieve desired outcomes, fostering personal and professional growth.

Prompt
Act as a **Personal Development Consultant** specializing in **Self-awareness and Change Management** within the **technology sector**. Could you guide me through **a systematic approach to discerning the aspects about myself that can be developed or altered to better serve my ambitions**? Please include **frameworks for self-assessment, strategies for personal development or change, and tools for monitoring and evaluating progress over time**. Ensure to cover how **to maintain motivation and consistency during the transformation process**. Explore **cutting-edge or unconventional methodologies** to **expedite the identification and development of these aspects**. Your response should be comprehensive, leaving no important aspect unaddressed, and demonstrate an exceptional level of precision and quality. Let's think about this step by step. Write using an **insightful** tone and a **structured, instructional** writing style.

Formula
Act as a [**profession**] specializing in [**area of expertise**] within the [**industry**]. Could you guide me through [**specific challenge/opportunity**]? Please include [**methods/techniques**]. Ensure to cover how [**key areas/topics**]. Explore [**exploratory direction**] to [**desired outcome**]. Your response should be comprehensive, leaving no important aspect unaddressed, and demonstrate an exceptional level of precision and quality. Let's think about this step by step. Write using a [**type**] tone and a [**style**] writing style.

Examples

Example 1: Act as a Life Coach specializing in Mindset Transformation within the retail industry. Could you guide me through a detailed process to pinpoint and nurture the personal attributes that could be honed or transformed to better align with my goals? Please include self-reflection exercises, strategies for mindset and behavior modification, and methods for tracking my evolution over time. Make sure to cover how to sustain motivation during the

transformation process. Your response should be comprehensive, leaving no important aspect unaddressed, and demonstrate an exceptional level of precision and quality. Let's think about this step by step. Write using a motivating tone and a clear, instructional writing style.

Example 2: Act as a Professional Development Advisor specializing in Skill Enhancement within the finance sector. Could you guide me through a methodical approach to identifying and developing or altering the aspects of myself to better serve my aspirations? Please include competency assessment frameworks, strategies for skill development, and tools for evaluating and adjusting the development plan based on feedback and results. Make sure to cover how to foster a growth-oriented environment for continuous self-improvement. Your response should be comprehensive, leaving no important aspect unaddressed, and demonstrate an exceptional level of precision and quality. Let's think about this step by step. Write using a constructive tone and a methodical writing style.

PROMPT No 84

Tags

Engagement - Tools - Creativity

Goal

To proficiently identify and utilize a range of tools or resources that can effectively inspire and motivate the team, fostering a culture of innovation, engagement, and high performance.

Prompt

Act as a **Motivational Strategist** specializing in **Team Inspiration** within the **advertising industry**. Could you guide me through **the various tools or resources I could employ to significantly inspire my team**? Please include **both conventional and digital tools, methodologies for gauging their effectiveness, and strategies for integrating them into our daily operations**. Ensure to cover how **to tailor these tools or resources** to **the diverse needs and preferences of my team members**. Venture into novel or avant-garde insights that could provide a fresh perspective or ignite creativity among the team. Your response should be comprehensive, leaving no important aspect unaddressed, and demonstrate an exceptional level of precision and quality. Let's think about this step by step. Write using an **engaging** tone and a **well-organized, instructional** writing style.

Formula

Act as a **[profession]** specializing in **[area of expertise]** within the **[industry]**. Could you guide me through **[specific challenge/opportunity]**? Please include **[methods/techniques]**. Make sure to cover how **[key areas/topics]**. Ensure to cover how **[exploratory direction]** to **[desired outcome]**. Venture into novel or avant-garde insights that could provide a fresh perspective or ignite creativity among the team. Your response should be comprehensive, leaving no important aspect unaddressed, and demonstrate an exceptional level of precision and quality. Let's think about this step by step. Write using a **[type]** tone and a **[style]** writing style.

Examples

Example 1: Act as a Leadership Coach specializing in Employee Engagement within the healthcare sector. Could you guide me through identifying and leveraging various tools or resources to motivate and inspire my team? Please include motivational frameworks, digital engagement platforms, and strategies for creating an inspiring work environment. Make sure to cover how to adapt these resources to align with the unique personalities and aspirations of my team members. Your response should be comprehensive, leaving no important aspect

unaddressed, and demonstrate an exceptional level of precision and quality. Let's think about this step by step. Write using a motivating tone and a structured, instructional writing style.

Example 2: Act as an Innovation Consultant specializing in Creative Stimuli within the design industry. Could you guide me through discovering and employing diverse tools or resources to spark inspiration and drive innovation among my team? Please include brainstorming tools, creative workshops, and digital platforms for sharing inspirational content. Make sure to cover how to measure the impact of these tools on the team's creativity and engagement. Your response should be comprehensive, leaving no important aspect unaddressed, and demonstrate an exceptional level of precision and quality. Let's think about this step by step. Write using a stimulating tone and a clear, instructional writing style.

PROMPT No 85

Tags

Reflective - Resourcefulness - Collaboration

Goal

To adeptly facilitate a reflective process for the team to identify, appreciate, and optimize their most valuable resources, thereby enhancing resourcefulness, collaboration, and overall productivity.

Prompt

Act as a **Resource Recognition Advisor** specializing in **Team Reflection** within the **renewable energy industry**. Could you guide me through **a thorough process to assist my team in reflecting upon and recognizing their most precious resources**? Please include **reflective exercises, identification methodologies, and strategies to leverage these resources effectively**. Ensure to cover how **to cultivate an ongoing awareness and appreciation of individual and collective resources**. Venture into innovative or unorthodox approaches that could unveil overlooked resources. Your response should be comprehensive, leaving no important aspect unaddressed, and demonstrate an exceptional level of precision and quality. Let's think about this step by step. Write using an **insightful** tone and a **structured, instructional** writing style.

Formula

Act as a **[profession]** specializing in **[area of expertise]** within the **[industry]**. Could you guide me through **[specific challenge/opportunity]**? Please include **[methods/techniques]**. Ensure to cover how **[key areas/topics]**. Venture into innovative or unorthodox approaches that could unveil overlooked resources. Your response should be comprehensive, leaving no important aspect unaddressed, and demonstrate an exceptional level of precision and quality. Let's think about this step by step. Write using a **[type]** tone and a **[style]** writing style.

Examples

Example 1: Act as a Resource Optimization Coach specializing in Reflective Practices within the manufacturing sector. Could you guide me through an in-depth process to help my team reflect on and value their most crucial resources? Please include guided reflection sessions, resource-mapping techniques, and strategies for resource optimization. Make sure to cover how to foster a culture of continuous reflection and resource appreciation. Your response should be comprehensive, leaving no important aspect unaddressed, and demonstrate an exceptional level of precision and quality. Let's think about this step by step. Write using a contemplative tone and a step-by-step instructional writing style.

Example 2: Act as a Team Development Consultant specializing in Resource Awareness within the pharmaceutical industry. Could you guide me through a comprehensive strategy to aid my team in recognizing and harnessing their most significant resources? Please include self-assessment tools, team discussions, and practices for effective resource allocation. Make sure to cover how to maintain an ongoing dialogue around resource identification and maximization. Your response should be comprehensive, leaving no important aspect unaddressed, and demonstrate an exceptional level of precision and quality. Let's think about this step by step. Write using a constructive tone and a clear, instructional writing style.

SELF-ASSESSMENT

PROMPT No 86

Leadership - Persuasion - Executive

To acquire actionable strategies, techniques, and frameworks for enhancing persuasion skills, with the objective of effectively influencing and leading a team in a business environment.

As an **Executive Leadership Coach** in the **technology sector**, could you provide a comprehensive guide on the steps **I** need to take to improve my **persuasion skills** for **influencing and leading my team**? Please include both **theoretical foundations and practical applications**. Break down the guide into **key components**, and substantiate each with **empirical evidence and case studies**. Explore unconventional solutions and alternative perspectives. Let's dissect this carefully. Write using an **authoritative** tone and a **structured** writing style.

As a **[profession]** in the **[industry]**, could you provide a comprehensive guide on the steps **[I/**Name/Role**]** need to take to improve my **[skillset]** for **[contextual challenge/opportunity]** in **[my/their]** **[team/group/department]**? Please include both **[theoretical foundations/practical applications]**. Break down the guide into **[key components]**, and substantiate each with **[empirical evidence/case studies]**. Explore unconventional solutions and alternative perspectives. Let's dissect this carefully. Write using a **[type]** tone and **[style]** writing style.

Example 1: As a Business Mentor in the healthcare industry, could you provide a comprehensive guide on the steps a project manager needs to take to improve their persuasion skills for influencing and leading their software development team? Please include both psychological theories and real-world applications. Segment the guide into crucial elements, and validate each with statistical data and industry-specific examples. Delve into uncharted territories and groundbreaking concepts. Let's examine each dimension meticulously. Write using a focused tone and a concise writing style.

Example 2: As a Leadership Development Consultant in the retail sector, could you provide a comprehensive guide on the steps I need to take to improve my persuasion skills for influencing and leading my sales team? Please include both ethical considerations and tactical maneuvers. Dissect the guide into fundamental principles, and corroborate each with scholarly articles and successful case studies. Unearth hidden gems and non-traditional methods. Let's tackle this in a phased manner. Write using a balanced tone and a nuanced writing style.

PROMPT No 87

Engagement - Passions - Cohesion

Goal

To equip leaders with a multi-faceted approach that fosters a culture of open sharing and engagement among team members, specifically focusing on the communication of individual passions within their professional lives, thereby enhancing team cohesion and motivation.

Prompt

Act as a **Communication Coach** specializing in the **banking industry**. Could you outline a **structured** strategy for **facilitating** an environment where my **colleagues** can **openly share** what they are **passionate about** in their **professional lives**? Include **actionable steps, communication exercises, and best practices** that **facilitate** this **open sharing**. Let's methodically dissect each component. Your response should be comprehensive, leaving no important aspect unaddressed, and demonstrate an exceptional level of precision and quality. Write using an **encouraging** tone and a **persuasive** writing style.

Formula

Act as a [profession] specializing in the [industry]. Could you outline a [structured/comprehensive] strategy for [facilitating/creating] an environment where my [colleagues/team members] can [openly share/discuss] what they are [passionate about/interested in] in their [professional lives/careers]? Include [actionable steps/communication exercises/best practices] that [facilitate/enable] this [open sharing/engagement]. Let's methodically dissect each component. Your response should be [comprehensive/thorough], leaving no important aspect unaddressed, and demonstrate an [exceptional/high] level of [precision/quality]. Write using a [type] tone and [style] writing style.

Examples

Example 1: Act as a Team Engagement Specialist specializing in the healthcare industry. Could you provide a comprehensive guide for creating a space where my colleagues can discuss their professional passions? Include team-building activities and ice-breaker exercises that can be used to facilitate this process. Let's sequentially address each element. Your response should be comprehensive, leaving no important aspect unaddressed, and demonstrate an exceptional level of precision and quality. Write using an inclusive tone and a collaborative writing style.

Example 2: Act as a Leadership Development Consultant specializing in the finance sector. Could you delineate a structured approach for enabling an environment where my team members can openly share their career interests? Include guidelines for structured team meetings and one-on-one sessions as venues for this sharing. Let's tackle this in a phased manner. Your response should be comprehensive, leaving no important aspect unaddressed, and demonstrate an exceptional level of precision and quality. Write using an inspirational tone and an authoritative writing style.

PROMPT No 88

Tags

Communication - Observational - Strategies

Goal

To acquire a multifaceted, actionable guide on indirect methods for gaining a deeper understanding of a boss's desires and vision for the future, with the aim of aligning team efforts and individual contributions more effectively in a business setting.

Prompt

As a **Corporate Communication Expert** in the **technology sector**, could you provide a comprehensive guide on indirect strategies **I** can employ to gain a deeper insight into **my** boss's desires for the future without directly asking **her**? Please include both **observational techniques and analytical tools**. Segment the guide into **specific categories**, and substantiate each with **empirical data and scholarly references**. Explore unconventional approaches and diverse viewpoints. Let's dissect this carefully. Write using an **analytical** tone and a **structured** writing style.

Formula

As a **[profession]** in the **[industry]**, could you provide a comprehensive guide on indirect strategies **[I/Name/Role]** can employ to gain a deeper insight into **[my/their]** boss's desires for the future without directly asking [him/her/them]? Please include both **[observational techniques/analytical tools]**. Segment the guide into **[specific categories]**, and substantiate each with **[empirical data/scholarly references]**. Explore unconventional approaches and diverse viewpoints. Let's dissect this carefully. Write using a **[type]** tone and **[style]** writing style.

Examples

Example 1: As a Human Resources Consultant in the healthcare industry, could you provide a comprehensive guide on indirect strategies a department head can employ to gain a deeper insight into their director's desires for the future without directly asking him? Please include both body language cues and data analytics. Divide the guide into key areas, and validate each with psychological studies and industry reports. Investigate unexpected avenues and creative pathways. Let's examine each dimension meticulously. Write using a focused tone and a concise writing style.

Example 2: As a Leadership Development Consultant in the retail sector, could you provide a comprehensive guide on indirect strategies I can employ to gain a deeper insight into my boss's desires for the future without directly asking her? Please include both social listening techniques and performance metrics. Break the guide into actionable steps, and corroborate each with market trends and academic literature. Unearth hidden gems and non-traditional methods. Let's tackle this in a phased manner. Write using a balanced tone and a nuanced writing style.

SKILLS

PROMPT No 89

Tags

Benchmarking - Development - Prioritization

Goal

To meticulously delineate and acquire the requisite new skills aligned with achieving specified key performance indicators or professional aspirations, thereby enhancing competency, performance, and career progression.

Prompt

Act as a **Professional Development Strategist** specializing in **Skill Gap Analysis** within the **telecommunications industry**. Could you guide me through **a thorough**

methodology to identify the specific new skills I need to acquire to meet my key performance indicators or professional goals? Please include **skill assessment tools, industry benchmarking, and personalized development plans**. Ensure to cover how **to prioritize these skills based on immediate and long-term objectives**. Explore **innovative approaches** to **skill acquisition that may expedite the attainment of my goals**. Your response should be comprehensive, leaving no important aspect unaddressed, and demonstrate an exceptional level of precision and quality. Let's think about this step by step. Write using a **structured** tone and a **strategic, actionable** writing style.

Act as a **[profession]** specializing in **[area of expertise]** within the **[industry]**. Could you guide me through **[specific challenge/opportunity]**? Please include **[methods/techniques]**. Ensure to cover how **[key areas/topics]**. Explore **[exploratory direction]** to **[desired outcome]**. Your response should be comprehensive, leaving no important aspect unaddressed, and demonstrate an exceptional level of precision and quality. Let's think about this step by step. Write using a **[type]** tone and a **[style]** writing style.

Example 1: Act as a Career Advancement Consultant specializing in Skill Identification within the finance sector. Could you guide me through a rigorous process to pinpoint the specific new skills I need to adopt to reach my key performance indicators or professional ambitions? Please include competency evaluations, industry skill standards, and tailored learning pathways. Make sure to cover how to align skill development with organizational objectives. Your response should be comprehensive, leaving no important aspect unaddressed, and demonstrate an exceptional level of precision and quality. Let's think about this step by step. Write using a diagnostic tone and a roadmap-oriented writing style.

Example 2: Act as a Professional Growth Analyst specializing in Performance-Driven Skill Development within the manufacturing sector. Could you guide me through a meticulous approach to determining the specific new skills I require to fulfill my key performance indicators or professional goals? Please include skill gap analyses, peer benchmarking, and actionable development plans. Make sure to cover how to measure the impact of newly acquired skills on performance metrics. Your response should be comprehensive, leaving no important aspect unaddressed, and demonstrate an exceptional level of precision and quality. Let's think about this step by step. Write using a solution-focused tone and a step-by-step instructional writing style.

PROMPT No 90

Prioritization - Effectiveness - Diagnostics

To provide a robust framework that enables professionals to identify and prioritize new skills for improvement, thereby enhancing their effectiveness and adaptability in their respective roles.

Act as a **Talent Development Specialist** specializing in the **manufacturing industry**. Could you **outline** a **methodical approach** for **identifying** and **prioritizing new** skills I need to **improve** on to become **more effective** in my **role**? Include d**iagnostic tools, actionable strategies, and key performance indicators** for **tracking progress**. Let's think about this **step by step**. Write using a **strategic** tone and a **forward-thinking** writing style.

Act as a **[profession]** specializing in the **[industry]**. Could you **[outline/delineate/provide]** a **[methodical/systematic/structured]** **[approach/methodology/plan]** for **[identifying/ascertaining/determining]** and **[prioritizing/ranking/organizing]** **[new/emerging/essential]** skills I need to **[improve/enhance/develop]** to become **[more effective/more efficient/more competent]** in my **[role/position/job]**? Include **[diagnostic tools/assessment methods/questionnaires]**, **[actionable strategies/practical steps/improvement plans]**, and **[key performance indicators/metrics/evaluation criteria]** for **[tracking/monitoring/assessing]** **[progress/development/improvement]**. Let's **[think about this step by step/systematically explore each facet]**. Write using a **[type]** tone and **[style]** writing style.

Example 1: Act as a Career Advisor specializing in the tech industry. Could you provide a systematic plan for ascertaining and ranking new skills I need to enhance to become more efficient in my job? Include assessment methods like SWOT analysis, practical steps for skill acquisition, and metrics for tracking development. Let's examine each dimension meticulously. Write using an analytical tone and a systematic writing style.

Example 2: Act as an Organizational Development Consultant specializing in the retail sector. Could you delineate a structured methodology for determining and organizing essential skills I need to develop to become more competent in my position? Include diagnostic tools like 360-degree feedback, actionable strategies for skill-building, and evaluation criteria for assessing improvement. Let's carefully evaluate each segment. Write using a consultative tone and an advisory writing style.

STRATEGIES

PROMPT No 91

Impediments - Proactive - Mitigation

To adeptly discern potential impediments that could thwart the progression and timely completion of tasks, through an exhaustive analysis employing proactive identification techniques, thereby fostering anticipatory measures to mitigate such hindrances, within the realm of Project Management in the construction industry.

As a **Risk Analysis Expert** specializing in **Proactive Obstacle Identification** within the **construction industry**, how can I adeptly discern potential impediments that could thwart the progression and timely completion of tasks? Please provide an in-depth elucidation on exhaustive analysis methodologies, proactive identification techniques, and **strategic foresight practices**. The discourse should extend to recommending anticipatory measures and **mitigation strategies** to address the identified hindrances, ensuring **uninterrupted task progression and adherence to timelines**. Your elaboration should be comprehensive, encapsulating all pertinent facets, and manifest a high degree of precision and quality.

As a **[Profession]** specializing in **[Specialization]** within the **[Industry],** how can I adeptly discern potential impediments that could thwart the progression and timely completion of tasks? Please provide an in-depth elucidation on exhaustive analysis methodologies, proactive identification techniques, and **[Additional Aspect]**. The discourse should extend to recommending anticipatory measures and **[Mitigation Strategies]** to address the identified hindrances, ensuring **[Desired Outcome].** Your elaboration should be comprehensive, encapsulating all pertinent facets, and manifest a high degree of precision and quality.

Examples

Example 1: As a Barrier Identification Specialist specializing in Proactive Problem-Solving within the software development industry, how can I adeptly discern potential impediments that could thwart the progression and timely completion of tasks? Please provide an in-depth elucidation on exhaustive analysis methodologies, proactive identification techniques, and agile response mechanisms. The discourse should extend to recommending anticipatory measures and adaptive strategies to address the identified hindrances, ensuring seamless task progression and punctual project delivery. Your elaboration should be comprehensive, encapsulating all pertinent facets, and manifest a high degree of precision and quality.

Example 2: As a Hurdle Recognition Analyst specializing in Anticipatory Management within the manufacturing industry, how can I adeptly discern potential impediments that could thwart the progression and timely completion of tasks? Please provide an in-depth elucidation on exhaustive analysis methodologies, proactive identification techniques, and resource allocation planning. The discourse should extend to recommending anticipatory measures and contingency plans to address the identified hindrances, ensuring continuous workflow and task execution within stipulated timelines. Your elaboration should be comprehensive, encapsulating all pertinent facets, and manifest a high degree of precision and quality.

STRENGTH

PROMPT No 92

Tags

Exhilaration - Strengths - Challenges

Goal

To provide leaders with a structured approach for facilitating team reflection on the specific strengths that are activated during exhilarating challenges, thereby enhancing self-awareness and optimizing performance.

Prompt

Act as a **Team Development Specialist** specializing in the **financial services industry**. Could you **outline** a **structured methodology** for helping my team **reflect** on the **strengths** they **leverage** when facing **exhilarating challenges**? Include **actionable exercises and assessment tools**. Let's methodically dissect each component. Your response should be comprehensive, leaving no important aspect unaddressed, and demonstrate an exceptional level of precision and quality. Write using an **analytical** tone and a **prescriptive** writing style.

Formula

Act as a **[profession]** specializing in the **[industry].** Could you **[outline/guide/develop]** a **[structured/step-by-step/comprehensive] [methodology/framework/approach]** for helping my team **[reflect/analyze/consider]** on the **[strengths/abilities/skills]** they

[leverage/utilize/employ] when facing **[exhilarating/challenging/demanding]** **[challenges/opportunities]**? Include **[actionable/practical/engaging]** **[exercises/activities/assessment tools]**. Let's methodically dissect each component. Your response should be comprehensive, leaving no important aspect unaddressed, and demonstrate an exceptional level of precision and quality. Write using a **[type]** tone and **[style]** writing style.

Example 1: Act as a Leadership Coach specializing in the healthcare sector. Could you guide me through a step-by-step approach for assisting my team in identifying the strengths they employ when facing high-stakes medical emergencies? Include practical activities and real-world scenarios for reflection. Let's sequentially address each element. Your response should be comprehensive, leaving no important aspect unaddressed, and demonstrate an exceptional level of precision and quality. Write using a compassionate tone and an instructive writing style.

Example 2: Act as an Organizational Psychologist specializing in the tech industry. Could you develop a comprehensive framework for helping my engineering team reflect on the skills they utilize when tackling complex coding challenges? Include engaging exercises and psychometric assessments. Let's tackle this in a phased manner. Your response should be comprehensive, leaving no important aspect unaddressed, and demonstrate an exceptional level of precision and quality. Write using an analytical tone and a data-driven writing style.

PROMPT No 93

Strengths - Engagement - Team-Dynamics

To guide leaders in assessing the specific strengths or sets of strengths that align well with their team's objectives and culture, thereby optimizing performance and engagement.

Act as a **business leadership coach** with a specialization in **team dynamics** for the **health care industry**. Could you guide me through **assessing if there are any specific strengths or sets of strengths that feel particularly right for my team**? Please include **assessment methods and key performance indicators (KPIs)**. Make sure to cover how **these strengths relate to current projects and team morale**. Unearth hidden gems and non-traditional methods. Let's dissect this in a structured manner. Write using a consultative tone and a detailed writing style.

Act as a **[profession]** with a specialization in **[area of expertise]** for the **[industry]**. Could you guide me through **[specific challenge/opportunity]**? Please include [methods/techniques]. Make sure to cover how **[key areas/topics]**. Unearth hidden gems and non-traditional methods to boost team morale and efficiency. Let's dissect this in a structured manner. Write using a **[type]** tone and **[style]** writing style.

Example 1: Act as a business leadership coach with a focus on team development for the tech industry. Can you assist me in identifying the core competencies that my development team should possess? Please incorporate proven assessment tools and relevant KPIs. Make sure to cover how these competencies can impact productivity and project timelines. Navigate through unexplored realms and revolutionary paradigms to improve teamwork. Let's explore this in a step-by-step fashion. Write with a consultative tone and a data-driven writing style.

Example 2: Act as an organizational psychologist with a specialization in employee engagement for the healthcare sector. How can I evaluate the innate strengths of my nursing staff to better allocate resources and tasks? Please mention psychometric tests and KPIs that would be useful. Make sure to cover how these strengths relate to patient care and employee satisfaction. Investigate unexpected avenues and creative pathways for elevating work quality and satisfaction. Let's analyze this systematically. Write using an empathetic tone and an evidence-based writing style.

PROMPT No 94

Tags

Ownership - Self-awareness - Strengths

Goal

To meticulously evaluate the degree of ownership and acknowledgement team members harbor towards their strengths, enabling a culture of self-awareness, self-efficacy, and continual professional growth.

Prompt

Act as an **Organizational Psychologist** specializing in **Strengths-Based Leadership** within the **retail industry**. Could you guide me through **a comprehensive methodology to assess the level of ownership my team feels for their strengths**? Please include **assessment tools, feedback mechanisms, and reflective exercises**. Ensure to cover how **to foster an environment where team members can openly recognize and leverage their strengths for personal and organizational betterment**. Explore **innovative approaches** to **reinforce self-awareness and promote a strengths-based culture**. Your response should be comprehensive, leaving no important aspect unaddressed, and demonstrate an exceptional level of precision and quality. Let's think about this step by step. Write using an **insightful** tone and a **methodical, actionable** writing style.

Formula

Act as a **[profession]** specializing in **[area of expertise]** within the **[industry]**. Could you guide me through **[specific challenge/opportunity]**? Please include **[methods/techniques]**. Ensure to cover how **[key areas/topics]**. Explore **[exploratory direction]** to **[desired outcome]**. Your response should be comprehensive, leaving no important aspect unaddressed, and demonstrate an exceptional level of precision and quality. Let's think about this step by step. Write using a **[type]** tone and a **[style]** writing style.

Examples

Example 1: Act as a Strengths Assessment Specialist specializing in Employee Engagement within the technology sector. Could you guide me through an in-depth process to gauge the level of ownership my team members feel towards their strengths? Please include self-assessment questionnaires, peer feedback, and strengths recognition workshops. Make sure to cover how to integrate strengths recognition into regular team interactions. Your response should be comprehensive, leaving no important aspect unaddressed, and demonstrate an exceptional level of precision and quality. Let's think about this step by step. Write using an encouraging tone and a systematic, step-by-step writing style.

Example 2: Act as a Talent Development Consultant specializing in Strengths-based Development within the automotive sector. Could you guide me through a well-rounded approach to assess the extent to which my team acknowledges and owns their strengths?

Please include strengths identification tools, constructive feedback sessions, and strategies for cultivating a strengths-focused mindset. Make sure to cover how to align team strengths with organizational objectives. Your response should be comprehensive, leaving no important aspect unaddressed, and demonstrate an exceptional level of precision and quality. Let's think about this step by step. Write using a motivational tone and a developmental, how-to-guide writing style.

PROMPT No 95

Exploration - Assets - Forward-thinking

To facilitate a deep-dive exploration with team members on leveraging their past assets and experiences as a substantial foundation for future endeavors, thereby promoting a culture of continuous learning, self-efficacy, and forward-thinking.

Act as a **Leadership Development Consultant** specializing in **Experiential Learning and Future Preparedness** within the **manufacturing sector**. Could you guide me through **a comprehensive process to explore with my team how they can leverage the assets from their past to support their future endeavors**? Please include **methodologies for identifying and articulating past assets, frameworks for aligning these assets with future goals, and strategies for fostering a culture of continuous learning and forward-thinking**. Ensure to cover how **to engage the team in a constructive dialogue and how to create a supportive environment for such reflective exercises**. Your response should encourage innovative thinking and possibly venture into novel approaches to leveraging past experiences for future growth. Let's think about this step by step. Write using an **inspiring** tone and a **solution-oriented** writing style.

Act as a **[profession]** specializing in **[area of expertise]** within the **[industry]**. Could you guide me through **[specific challenge/opportunity]**? Please include **[methods/techniques]**. Ensure to cover how **[key areas/topics]**. Your response should encourage innovative thinking and possibly venture into novel approaches to leveraging past experiences for future growth. Let's think about this step by step. Write using a **[type]** tone and a **[style]** writing style.

Example 1: Act as a Career Transition Coach specializing in Leveraging Past Achievements within the retail sector. Could you guide me through a process to help my team identify and utilize their past assets and achievements to bolster their future endeavors? Please include self-reflection tools, group discussions frameworks, and strategies for aligning past assets with individual and team goals. Make sure to cover how to foster an environment that encourages sharing and collaboration. Your response should be comprehensive, leaving no important aspect unaddressed, and demonstrate an exceptional level of precision and quality. Let's think about this step by step. Write using a motivational tone and a collaborative writing style.

Example 2: Act as an Organizational Learning Expert specializing in Experiential Asset Identification within the technology sector. Could you guide me through a structured approach to engage my team in recognizing and articulating their past assets, and aligning them with our forward-looking organizational objectives? Please include methods for asset identification, techniques for constructive dialogue, and strategies for promoting a growth mindset. Make sure to cover how to track the impact of leveraging past assets on future endeavors. Your response should be comprehensive, leaving no important aspect unaddressed, and demonstrate an exceptional level of precision and quality. Let's think about this step by step. Write using an analytical tone and a strategic writing style.

PROMPT No 96

Tags
Overextension - Self-awareness - Diagnostics

Goal
To equip leaders with a robust framework for identifying scenarios where team members might overextend their strengths, potentially leading to counterproductivity or strain, and to cultivate an environment that fosters balanced utilization of strengths.

Prompt
Act as an **Organizational Behavior Specialist** specializing in **Strengths Optimization** within the **pharmaceutical industry**. Could you guide me through **a meticulous process to identify situations or circumstances when my team tends to push their strengths to their extreme, and how to mitigate any negative repercussions**? Please include **diagnostic tools, observational techniques, and behavioral indicators**. Make sure to cover **strategies for fostering self-awareness among team members and creating a culture that encourages balanced utilization of strengths**. Delve into innovative methods for maintaining a harmonious balance between leveraging strengths and avoiding overextension. Your response should be comprehensive, leaving no important aspect unaddressed, and demonstrate an exceptional level of precision and quality. Let's think about this step by step. Write using a **reflective** tone and a **solutions-focused** writing style.

Formula
Act as a **[profession]** specializing in **[area of expertise]** within the **[industry]**. Could you guide me through **[specific challenge/opportunity]**? Please include **[methods/techniques]**. Make sure to cover **[key areas/topics]**. Delve into innovative methods for maintaining a harmonious balance between leveraging strengths and avoiding overextension. Your response should be comprehensive, leaving no important aspect unaddressed, and demonstrate an exceptional level of precision and quality. Let's think about this step by step. Write using a **[type]** tone and a **[style]** writing style.

Examples

Example 1: Act as a Performance Management Expert specializing in Strengths-Based Leadership within the automotive sector. Could you guide me through identifying situations where my team might be pushing their strengths too far, and provide strategies to encourage a balanced approach? Please include assessment instruments, team discussion frameworks, and feedback mechanisms. Make sure to cover how to foster a supportive environment for balanced strengths utilization. Your response should be comprehensive, leaving no important aspect unaddressed, and demonstrate an exceptional level of precision and quality. Let's think about this step by step. Write using an empowering tone and an instructional writing style.

Example 2: Act as a Leadership Development Consultant specializing in Balanced Strengths Utilization within the financial services sector. Could you guide me through a methodical approach to discern when my team tends to overextend their strengths and how to guide them towards a more balanced application? Please include self-reflection exercises, peer feedback processes, and coaching techniques. Make sure to cover how to establish a culture that values balanced strengths utilization. Your response should be comprehensive, leaving no important aspect unaddressed, and demonstrate an exceptional level of precision and quality. Let's think about this step by step. Write using a constructive tone and a coaching-focused writing style.

PROMPT No 97

Transparency - Authenticity - Investigation

Goal

To develop a nuanced understanding and strategy for identifying circumstances where team members might feel compelled to conceal or underplay their strengths, thereby enabling a culture that encourages transparency, self-expression, and the optimal utilization of individual and collective strengths.

Prompt

Act as an **Organizational Development Specialist** specializing in **Strengths Transparency** within the **technology sector**. Could you guide me through **an exhaustive exploration of situations or contexts in which my team feels tempted to hide or downplay their strengths**? Please include **investigative methodologies, psychological insights, and communication frameworks**. Ensure to cover **strategies for creating a supportive environment that encourages the open recognition and utilization of strengths**. Delve into **both conventional and unconventional approaches to fostering an organizational culture that values authenticity and the diverse capabilities of each team member**. Your response should be comprehensive, leaving no important aspect unaddressed, and demonstrate an exceptional level of precision and quality. Let's think about this step by step. Write using an **engaging** tone and an **exploratory** writing style.

Formula

Act as a **[profession]** specializing in **[area of expertise]** within the **[industry]**. Could you guide me through **[specific challenge/opportunity]**? Please include **[methods/techniques]**. Ensure to cover **[key areas/topics]**. Delve into **[additional exploration]**. Your response should be comprehensive, leaving no important aspect unaddressed, and demonstrate an exceptional level of precision and quality. Let's think about this step by step. Write using a **[type]** tone and a **[style]** writing style.

Examples

Example 1: Act as a Talent Development Strategist specializing in Authentic Leadership within the retail sector. Could you guide me through discerning scenarios in which my team may feel inclined to mask or minimize their strengths? Please include identification tools, psychological factors, and structured dialogues. Make sure to cover how to promote a culture of authenticity and strengths-based collaboration. Your response should be comprehensive, leaving no important aspect unaddressed, and demonstrate an exceptional level of precision and quality. Let's think about this step by step. Write using an enlightening tone and a dialogue-facilitating writing style.

Example 2: Act as a Corporate Culture Consultant specializing in Strengths Acknowledgment within the hospitality sector. Could you guide me through unraveling the contexts in which my team may opt to conceal or downplay their strengths? Please include observational techniques, feedback systems, and inclusivity initiatives. Make sure to cover how to foster an atmosphere that embraces diverse strengths and the constructive expression of self. Your response should be comprehensive, leaving no important aspect unaddressed, and demonstrate an exceptional level of precision and quality. Let's think about this step by step. Write using a nurturing tone and an action-oriented writing style.

PROMPT No 98

Misalignment - Assessment - Realignment

Goal

To methodically assess and reflect on the ramifications of any misalignment between team members' roles and their strengths, aiming to generate actionable insights that will guide realignment strategies, enhance job satisfaction, and boost team performance.

Prompt

Act as an **Organizational Alignment Specialist** with a focus on **Strengths-Based Development** within the **hospitality industry**. Could you guide me through **a detailed analysis to reflect on the impact of any misalignment between my team's roles and their strengths**? Please include **assessment methodologies, reflective discussions, and impact analysis techniques**. Ensure to cover how **to derive actionable insights from these reflections to realign roles with strengths, along with strategies to measure the improvements post realignment**. Examine **both the immediate and long-term impacts of such misalignments and the benefits of addressing them**. Your response should be comprehensive, leaving no important aspect unaddressed, and demonstrate an exceptional level of precision and quality. Let's think about this step by step. Write using an **analytical** tone and a **structured** writing style.

Formula

Act as a **[profession]** with a focus on **[area of expertise]** within the **[industry]**. Could you guide me through **[specific challenge/opportunity]**? Please include **[methods/techniques]**. Ensure to cover how **[key areas/topics]**. Examine **[additional exploration]**. Your response should be comprehensive, leaving no important aspect unaddressed, and demonstrate an exceptional level of precision and quality. Let's think about this step by step. Write using a **[type]** tone and a **[style]** writing style.

Examples

Example 1: Act as a Team Dynamics Analyst specializing in Role-Strengths Alignment within the retail sector. Could you guide me through an in-depth examination to reflect on the repercussions of any misalignment between my team's roles and their strengths? Please include evaluation tools, reflective discussions, and post-assessment strategies. Ensure to cover how to transition from reflection to action in realigning roles with strengths to enhance job satisfaction and team productivity. Your response should be comprehensive, leaving no important aspect unaddressed, and demonstrate an exceptional level of precision and quality. Let's think about this step by step. Write using a constructive tone and a results-driven writing style.

Example 2: Act as a Strengths Alignment Consultant specializing in Organizational Effectiveness within the automotive sector. Could you guide me through a comprehensive exploration to understand the impact of any misalignment between my team's roles and their strengths? Please include diagnostic assessments, group reflection sessions, and strategies to bridge the identified gaps. Ensure to cover how to engage the team in this realignment process and measure the success of realignment initiatives. Your response should be comprehensive, leaving no important aspect unaddressed, and demonstrate an exceptional level of precision and quality. Let's think about this step by step. Write using an insightful tone and a collaborative writing style.

PROMPT No 99

Tags

Assumptions - Decision-Making - Risk Management

Goal

To meticulously delineate and implement a well-structured, evidence-based approach aimed at minimizing the propensity for erroneous assumptions and misguided actions, thereby fostering a culture of informed decision-making and enhanced performance.

Prompt

As a **Decision Analysis Expert** specializing in **Risk Minimization** within the **Financial Services industry**, how can I methodically outline and enact a robust, evidence-driven approach aimed at curtailing the tendency for incorrect assumptions and misguided actions? I am seeking a comprehensive elucidation on a systematic framework encompassing the **identification, assessment, and rectification** of potential misjudgments, along with insights on promoting a culture of **analytical thinking and informed decision-making**. The discourse should also articulate the consequential impact of such an approach on **organizational performance, risk management, and stakeholder confidence**. Your explication should be exhaustive, addressing every pivotal aspect with an exceptional degree of precision and quality.

Formula

As a **[Profession]** specializing in **[Specialization]** within the **[Industry]**, how can I methodically outline and enact a robust, evidence-driven approach aimed at curtailing the tendency for incorrect assumptions and misguided actions? I am seeking a comprehensive elucidation on a systematic framework encompassing the **[Identification/Assessment/Rectification]** of potential misjudgments, along with insights on promoting a culture of **[Analytical/Critical Thinking Aspect]** and **[Informed Decision-Making/Other Relevant Aspect]**. The discourse should also articulate the consequential impact of such an approach on **[Organizational Performance/Risk Management/Stakeholder Confidence or Other Relevant Outcome]**. Your explication should be exhaustive, addressing every pivotal aspect with an exceptional degree of precision and quality.

Examples

Example 1: As an Analytical Prudence Advisor specializing in Cognitive Bias Mitigation within the Information Technology industry, how can I methodically outline and enact a robust, evidence-driven approach aimed at curtailing the tendency for incorrect assumptions and misguided actions? I am seeking a comprehensive elucidation on a systematic framework encompassing the identification, assessment, and rectification of potential misjudgments, along with insights on promoting a culture of data-driven analysis and informed decision-making. The discourse should also articulate the consequential impact of such an approach on project success rates, error reduction, and client satisfaction. Your explication should be exhaustive, addressing every pivotal aspect with an exceptional degree of precision and quality.

Example 2: As a Risk Assessment Specialist specializing in Decision Integrity within the Pharmaceutical industry, how can I methodically outline and enact a robust, evidence-driven approach aimed at curtailing the tendency for incorrect assumptions and misguided actions? I am seeking a comprehensive elucidation on a systematic framework encompassing the identification, assessment, and rectification of potential misjudgments, along with insights on promoting a culture of scientific skepticism and informed decision-making. The discourse should also articulate the consequential impact of such an approach on regulatory compliance, product safety, and public trust. Your explication should be exhaustive, addressing every pivotal aspect with an exceptional degree of precision and quality.

PROMPT No 100

Tags

Patience - Empathy - Reflective

Goal

To facilitate a reflective process for my team that helps identify the support and resources required to nurture patience in their interactions with customers or other stakeholders, thereby enhancing stakeholder satisfaction and fostering positive relations.

Prompt

Act as a **Patient Experience Specialist** with a specialization in **Interpersonal Skills Training** within the **retail industry**. Could you guide me through **an introspective exercise to help my team reflect on the support they need to cultivate patience in their interactions with customers or other stakeholders**? Please include **reflective frameworks, empathy-building exercises, and training modules on patience**. Make sure to cover how to create a supportive environment that encourages patience and understanding, and how **to measure the impact of these initiatives on stakeholder satisfaction**. Delve into **innovative solutions and alternative perspectives to enrich these interactions and meet the unique challenges posed by impatient or demanding stakeholders**. Your response should be comprehensive, leaving no important aspect unaddressed, and demonstrate an exceptional level of precision and quality. Let's think about this step by step. Write using a **nurturing** tone and a **facilitative** writing style.

Formula

Act as a **[profession]** with a specialization in **[area of expertise]** within the **[industry]**. Could you guide me through **[specific challenge/opportunity]**? Please include **[methods/techniques]**. Make sure to cover how **[key areas/topics]**. Delve into **[additional exploration]**. Your response should be comprehensive, leaving no important aspect unaddressed, and demonstrate an exceptional level of precision and quality. Let's think about this step by step. Write using a **[type]** tone and a **[style]** writing style.

Examples

Example 1: Act as a Communication Coach with a specialization in Emotional Intelligence within the hospitality industry. Could you guide me through a reflective journey to help my team identify the support they require to foster patience in their interactions with guests or other stakeholders? Please include self-awareness activities, emotion regulation techniques, and role-play scenarios. Make sure to cover how to establish a culture of patience, and ways to evaluate the effectiveness of these initiatives on guest satisfaction. Explore pioneering approaches to enhancing patience and understanding in high-pressure or demanding scenarios. Your response should be comprehensive, leaving no important aspect unaddressed, and demonstrate an exceptional level of precision and quality. Let's think about this step by step. Write using an empathetic tone and an instructive writing style.

Example 2: Act as a Stakeholder Relations Expert with a specialization in Conflict Resolution within the telecommunications industry. Could you guide me through a contemplative process to help my team discern the support they need to nurture patience in their interactions with customers or other stakeholders? Please include mindfulness exercises, customer service training modules, and feedback gathering mechanisms. Make sure to cover how to create an environment that celebrates patience and positive stakeholder interactions, and how to track the improvements in stakeholder relations over time. Investigate novel solutions and alternative viewpoints to enrich these interactions and overcome the challenges posed by demanding or dissatisfied stakeholders. Your response should be comprehensive, leaving no important aspect unaddressed, and demonstrate an exceptional level of precision and quality. Let's think about this step by step. Write using a diplomatic tone and a collaborative writing style.

PROMPT No 101

System Analysis - KPIs - Scalability

To provide organizational leaders, project managers, and individual contributors with an all-encompassing methodology for identifying the structures or systems that are instrumental in achieving specific projects or goals, thereby ensuring efficient execution and success.

Act as a **Systems Analyst** with a specialization in **organizational structures** in the **telecommunications industry**. Could you guide me through **a comprehensive approach to identify the structures or systems that will aid in achieving specific projects or goals**? Please include **frameworks for system analysis, key performance indicators, and scalability considerations**. Make sure to cover how **to integrate these structures into existing workflows and how to measure their effectiveness**. Investigate unconventional **organizational models** and cutting-edge **technologies** to **optimize project outcomes.** Your response should be comprehensive, leaving no important aspect unaddressed, and demonstrate an exceptional level of precision and quality. Let's think about this step by step. Write using an **evaluative** tone and a **systems analysis** style.

Act as a **[profession]** with a specialization in **[area of expertise]** in the **[industry]**. Could you guide me through **[specific challenge/opportunity]**? Please include **[methods/techniques]**. Make sure to cover how **[key areas/topics]**. Investigate unconventional **[area for innovation]** and cutting-edge **[technologies/methods]** to **[desired outcome]**. Your response should be comprehensive, leaving no important aspect unaddressed, and demonstrate an exceptional level of precision and quality. Let's think about this step by step. Write using a **[type]** tone and **[style]** writing style.

Example 1: Act as a Business Process Consultant with a specialization in workflow optimization in the healthcare industry. Could you guide me through a structured approach to identify the systems or structures that will facilitate the achievement of our patient care goals? Please include process mapping, performance metrics, and compliance considerations. Make sure to cover how to align these systems with healthcare regulations and staff capabilities. Explore the potential of telemedicine and AI diagnostics to enhance patient care. Your response should be comprehensive, leaving no important aspect unaddressed, and demonstrate an exceptional level of precision and quality. Let's think about this step by step. Write using a diagnostic tone and a process improvement style.

Example 2: Act as an IT Architect with a specialization in infrastructure design in the finance sector. Could you guide me through a plan to determine the systems or structures that will aid in achieving our data security goals? Please include network design, security protocols, and disaster recovery plans. Make sure to cover how to integrate these structures with existing IT assets and how to conduct regular security audits. Delve into blockchain solutions and quantum encryption methods to fortify data security. Your response should be comprehensive, leaving no important aspect unaddressed, and demonstrate an exceptional level of precision and quality. Let's think about this step by step. Write using a prescriptive tone and a technical blueprint style.

PROMPT No 102

Tags
Resilience - Communication - Emotional Intelligence

Goal
To develop a well-rounded and actionable plan for navigating disappointment in professional contexts, encompassing emotional intelligence, strategic communication, and resilience-building techniques tailored to the unique dynamics of your team.

Prompt
As a **human resources manager** specializing in **organizational behavior** within the **healthcare industry**, provide an exhaustive and meticulous examination, incorporating innovative insights and inventive strategies for **outlining various approaches your team can adopt for effectively dealing with disappointment—be it project failures, missed promotions, or team conflicts**. Additionally, elucidate how to embed these approaches into **ongoing training and team culture**.

Formula
As a [profession] specializing in [area of expertise/focus] within the [industry], provide an exhaustive and meticulous examination, incorporating innovative insights and inventive strategies for [outlining various strategies or approaches your team can adopt to effectively deal with disappointment—such as project failures, missed promotions, or team conflicts]. Additionally, elucidate how to embed these approaches into [ongoing training/team culture/organizational frameworks].

Examples
Example 1: As a sales director specializing in B2B solutions within the tech industry, provide an exhaustive and meticulous examination, incorporating innovative insights and inventive strategies, to devise strategies your team can employ to cope with the disappointment of lost accounts or missed sales targets. Additionally, elucidate how to integrate these approaches into quarterly reviews and training sessions. **Example 2:** As a team leader specializing in software development within the fintech sector, provide an exhaustive and meticulous examination, incorporating innovative

insights and inventive strategies, to highlight methods your engineers can use to navigate disappointments like code failures or unsuccessful product launches. Additionally, elucidate how to incorporate these approaches into your team's agile development process.

VALUES

PROMPT No 103

Tags
Self-reflection - Values - Identity

Goal
To gain specific and detailed recommendations on effective methods for a team to engage in self-reflection and articulate their core values, which serve as guiding principles in shaping their identity.

Prompt
As a **Life Coach**, adopting an **empathetic and insightful tone**, could you offer specific and detailed recommendations on effective methods for **my team and me** to engage in **self-reflection**? Additionally, please provide insights on how we can **articulate our core values, which serve as guiding principles in shaping our identity**.

Formula
As a **[profession]**, adopting a **[tone of voice]**, could you offer specific and detailed recommendations on effective methods for **[my/their]** **[team/group/department]** to engage in **[desired outcome]**? Additionally, please provide insights on how we can **[contextual challenge/opportunity]**.

Examples
Example 1: As a Leadership Development Consultant, adopting a supportive and understanding tone, could you offer specific and detailed recommendations on effective methods for the marketing department to engage in self-reflection? Additionally, please provide insights on how they can articulate their core values, which serve as guiding principles in shaping their identity.
Example 2: As a Team Coach, adopting a motivational and inspiring tone, could you offer specific and detailed recommendations on effective methods for my sales team to engage in self-reflection? Additionally, please provide insights on how we can articulate our core values, which serve as guiding principles in shaping our identity.

PROMPT No 104

Tags
Alignment - CoreValues - Tangible

Goal
To gain a detailed and comprehensive understanding of specific and tangible actions that a team can take, regardless of how minor they may seem, to ensure complete alignment with their core values.

Prompt

As a **Leadership Development Consultant**, adopting a **supportive and encouraging tone**, could you provide some specific and tangible actions that **my team** can take, no matter how small, to ensure that they are completely aligned with their **core values**? Please provide a detailed and comprehensive response, considering all aspects of **this alignment**.

As a **[profession]**, adopting a **[tone of voice]**, could you provide some specific and tangible actions that **[my/their]** **[team/group/department]** can take, no matter how small, to ensure that they are completely aligned with their **[contextual challenge/opportunity]**? Please provide a detailed and comprehensive response, considering all aspects of **[desired outcome]**.

Example 1: As a Team Coach, adopting a motivational and positive tone, could you provide some specific and tangible actions that my sales team can take, no matter how small, to ensure that they are completely aligned with their sales targets? Please provide a detailed and comprehensive response, considering all aspects of this alignment.

Example 2: As a Human Resources Consultant, adopting a professional and clear tone, could you provide some specific and tangible actions that their department can take, no matter how small, to ensure that they are completely aligned with their departmental goals? Please provide a detailed and comprehensive response, considering all aspects of this alignment.

PROMPT No 105

Roadmap - Alignment - TeamValues

To gain insights on how to effectively utilize team values in creating a roadmap towards a particular goal or objective, enhancing team alignment and success.

As a **Leadership Development Consultant**, could you guide **me** on how I can effectively utilize the values of **my team** to create a satisfying and successful roadmap towards a **particular goal or objective**? I'm seeking this advice in a **solution-oriented and encouraging tone**, particularly considering the importance of **aligning team values with our objectives**.

As a **[profession]**, could you guide **[I/Name/Role]** on how **[I/they]** can effectively utilize the values of **[my/their]** **[team/group/department]** to create a satisfying and successful roadmap towards a **[goal/objective]**? **[I/They]** am/are seeking this advice in a **[tone of voice]**, particularly considering the importance of **[contextual challenge/opportunity]**.

Example 1: As a Business Coach, could you guide a department head on how they can effectively utilize the values of their team to create a satisfying and successful roadmap towards improving customer satisfaction? They are seeking this advice in a supportive and patient tone, particularly considering the importance of aligning team values with customer service goals.

Example 2: Could you guide me on how I can effectively utilize the values of my creative team to create a satisfying and successful roadmap towards completing our project on time?

As a Project Management Consultant, I'm seeking this advice in a clear and concise tone, particularly considering the importance of aligning team values with creative project deadlines.

PROMPT No 106

Dialogue - Leadership - Values

To facilitate leaders in initiating meaningful dialogues with their teams concerning the significance of values both individually and collectively. The discussions aim to instill a deeper understanding, commitment, and alignment of values that shape behaviors, decision-making processes, and overall team dynamics.

As a **Leadership Development Coach** with a specialization in **values and ethics** for the **software development industry**, could you guide me through **the process of conducting a thoughtful discussion with my team to explore the importance and significance of the values they hold**? Include **methods for initiating the conversation, kinds of questions to pose, techniques for creating a supportive environment for sharing, and potential next steps for action planning**. Ensure that the guide covers **how to integrate reflective practices and ethics-driven evaluations into team activities**. Introduce unique perspectives and future implications. Let's think about this step by step. Write using an **informative** tone and **factual** writing style.

As a **[profession]** with specialization in **[focus area]** for the **[industry]**, could you guide me through **[contextual challenge/opportunity]**? Include **[methods/techniques]**. Ensure that the guide covers **[tools/frameworks]**. Introduce unique perspectives and future implications. Let's think about this step by step. Write using a **[type]** tone and **[style]** writing style.

Example 1: As a Corporate Ethics Advisor specializing in workplace values for the retail sector, could you guide me through the best practices for encouraging my staff to reflect on the significance of customer service, teamwork, and integrity? Incorporate exercises for initiating the dialogue, probing questions that dig deeper, and approaches to celebrate and affirm value-based actions. Ensure that the guide elaborates on how to apply moral philosophy frameworks like consequentialism or deontological ethics in everyday work decisions. Consider innovative teaching methods and impactful opportunities. Let's break this down methodically. Write using an accessible tone and practical writing style.

Example 2: As a Business Consultant with a focus on company culture for the non-profit sector, could you walk me through the process for facilitating a discussion among my team members to reflect on the importance of social responsibility, collaboration, and individual initiative? Include guidelines for setting the stage, in-depth questions that elicit honest reflections, and follow-up activities to keep the values alive. Make sure the guide includes criteria for value-based performance reviews and ways to memorialize shared values in the organization. Present new viewpoints and untapped future prospects. Let's analyze this incrementally. Write using a persuasive tone and a motivating writing style.

PROMPT No 107

Evaluation - Abilities - Talent

To gain insights on specific methods or approaches to accurately detect and evaluate any deficiencies in the abilities or expertise of team members, enhancing their development and performance.

Given the importance of **accurately detecting and evaluating team members' abilities**, as a **Talent Management Specialist** and in a **respectful and professional tone**, could you suggest specific methods or approaches **I** can utilize for **this purpose**?

Given the importance of **[contextual challenge/opportunity],** as a **[profession]** and in a **[tone of voice]**, could you suggest specific methods or approaches **[I/Name/Role]** can utilize for **[desired outcome]**?

Example 1: Given the importance of accurately detecting and evaluating project team members' abilities, as a Human Resources Consultant and in a clear and concise tone, could you suggest specific methods or approaches a project manager can utilize for this purpose?

Example 2: As a Performance Management Specialist, in a supportive and constructive tone, could you suggest specific methods or approaches I can utilize to accurately detect and evaluate any deficiencies in the abilities or expertise of my operations team members, especially given the importance of supervising and organizing production schedules in achieving our targets?

PROMPT No 108

Articulation - EmotionalIQ - SelfAwareness

To empower team members to self-identify weaknesses or areas for improvement and articulate them clearly. The discussion aims to foster an environment of self-awareness and personal responsibility, which should lead to actionable improvement plans. The end goal is to enhance overall team productivity, individual growth, and collective well-being.

As a **Leadership Development Coach** with a specialization in **self-awareness and emotional intelligence** for the **technology sector**, could you guide me through **the steps to encourage my team to independently identify and articulate their own weaknesses or areas needing improvement**? Please include **suggestions on how to introduce the concept, encourage individual reflection, and create a secure environment where team members are comfortable sharing their insights**. Ensure the guide covers **frameworks or tools that can be used for self-assessment**, as well **as methods for channeling these discoveries into actionable plans**. Introduce unique angles and future-forward opportunities. Let's think about this step by step. Write using an **informative** tone and **factual** writing style.

Formula

As a **[profession]** with a specialization in **[focus area]** for the **[industry]**, could you guide me through **[contextual challenge/opportunity]**? Please include **[techniques/methods/steps]**. Ensure the guide covers **[tools/frameworks/methods]**. Introduce unique angles and future-forward opportunities. Let's think about this step by step. Write using a **[type]** tone and **[style]** writing style.

Examples

Example 1: As a Career Development Specialist focusing on self-assessment for the healthcare industry, could you guide me through designing an exercise that allows my team to independently identify their skills gaps or areas of improvement? Please outline how to effectively introduce this concept in a team meeting, types of activities that encourage self-reflection, and ways to build a non-judgmental space. Ensure the guide includes established assessment tools like 360-degree feedback and SMART goals. Introduce unconventional methods and transformative opportunities. Let's break this down in detail. Write using an empathetic tone and a collaborative writing style.

Example 2: As a Mindfulness Coach specializing in workplace well-being for the financial services industry, could you guide me through the process of facilitating a session where my team can identify and verbalize their weaknesses in stress management? Include the appropriate way to introduce this sensitive topic, mindfulness exercises that aid self-reflection, and methods to ensure psychological safety. Make sure the guide incorporates techniques for converting self-discoveries into practical stress management plans. Introduce alternative perspectives and innovative solutions. Let's dissect this carefully. Write using a calm tone and reflective writing style.

PROMPT No 109

Tags

Overlooked - Management - Opportunities

Goal

To gain insights on potential overlooked aspects of a team's work that they may be unaware of or not fully considering, helping to prevent negative consequences or missed opportunities.

Prompt

Considering the potential for **overlooked aspects of work leading to negative consequences or missed opportunities**, as a **Management Consultant** and in a **clear and concise tone**, could you identify some areas of **my team's** work that they may be unaware of or not fully considering?

Formula

Considering the potential for **[contextual challenge/opportunity]**, as a **[profession]** and in a **[tone of voice]**, could you identify some areas of **[I/Name/Role]'s** **[team/group/department]'s** work that they may be unaware of or not fully considering?

Examples

Example 1: Considering the potential for overlooked aspects of project management leading to project delays or missed deadlines, as a Project Management Consultant and in a solution-oriented tone, could you identify some areas of a project team's work that they may be unaware of or not fully considering?

Example 2: As a Business Coach, in a professional and diplomatic tone, could you identify some areas of my sales team's work that they may be unaware of or not fully considering, especially considering the potential for overlooked aspects of customer relationship management leading to lost sales or customer dissatisfaction?

PROMPT No 110

Self-Improvement - Experience - Reflective

To gain insights on how to encourage a team to reflect on the missed opportunities or experiences due to not actively working on their areas of weakness, promoting self-improvement.

In the context of **encouraging self-improvement**, as an **Executive Coach** and in a **reflective and patient tone**, could you advise on how **I** could make **my team** reflect on the specific things they are giving up or failing to experience as a result of not actively working to improve their **areas of weakness**?

In the context of **[contextual challenge/opportunity]**, as a **[profession]** and in a **[tone of voice]**, could you advise on how **[I/Name/Role]** could make **[my/their] [team/group/department]** reflect on the specific things they are giving up or failing to experience as a result of not actively working to improve their **[areas of weakness/shortcomings]**?

Example 1: In the context of encouraging continuous learning, as a Learning and Development Specialist and in a supportive and understanding tone, could you advise on how a manager could make their team reflect on the specific things they are giving up or failing to experience as a result of not actively working to improve their skills gaps?
Example 2: As a Performance Coach, in an empathetic and respectful tone, could you advise on how I could make my public relationship team reflect on the specific opportunities they are missing out on as a result of not actively working to improve their areas of weakness, especially in the context of a public speaking skills?

PROMPT No 111

Performance - Qualities - Empowerment

To gain insights on the specific internal qualities or attributes to focus on developing within a team to enhance their overall performance.

Given the objective of **enhancing team performance**, as a **Performance Coach** and in an **empowering and constructive tone**, could you specify the **internal qualities or attributes I** should focus on developing within **my team**?

Given the objective of **[contextual challenge/opportunity]**, as a **[profession]** and in a **[tone of voice],** could you specify the **[qualities/attributes/skills] [I/Name/Role]** should focus on developing within **[my/their] [team/group/department]**?

Example 1: Given the objective of enhancing project team performance, as a Team Coach and in a supportive and encouraging tone, could you specify the internal qualities a project manager should focus on developing within their team?

Example 2: As a Leadership Development Facilitator, in an inspiring and motivating tone, could you specify the attributes I should focus on developing within my logistic team to improve their overall performance, especially given the objective of having better inventory management

Final Words

In the domain of coaching, mentoring, and leadership, navigating the complexities requires a disciplined approach. This book aims to be an instrumental guide, leveraging artificial intelligence and prompt engineering to provide actionable insights for those in any profession. I have presented a curated list of prompts, each serving a specific objective: to clarify roles, define leadership strategies, and optimize coaching techniques, to name a few.

The scope of this book goes beyond a mere compilation of prompts. My goal is to impart a strategic mindset for interpreting challenges as opportunities, seeing barriers as milestones for growth, and viewing the future as a dynamic environment that can be strategically managed.

For the reader who began with skepticism, I hope you conclude this book with a newfound confidence, equipped with a toolkit that elevates your professional standing. For the experienced practitioner, may the methods and strategies here serve to refine your existing approaches.

This journey, while individual in nature, is set against the backdrop of collective human experience. Artificial intelligence serves as a bridge to this collective wisdom, streamlining the path toward your professional and personal development objectives.

In summary, this book aims to leave you not just prepared but empowered. As you close this chapter and move forward in your career, be reminded that each decision and action point offers an opportunity for growth and leadership. This is not just preparation; it is empowerment for transformative impact.

The challenges you face should be viewed as opportunities for demonstrating your leadership and expertise. I encourage you to approach these with a strategic focus, grounded in the knowledge and insights you have gained from this book.

I wish you all the best.

Mauricio

PS. To leave your review of this book, please scan this QR code!

APPENDIXES

Appendix No 1

Sign-In to Chatbots

1,1. Chat GPT

Step 1: Visit ChatGPT on https://chat.openai.com/chat Click on "Sign Up" and then create your account.

Step 2: Verify your Account. You'd have to enter your details, verify your email and give an OTP you'll receive on your phone.

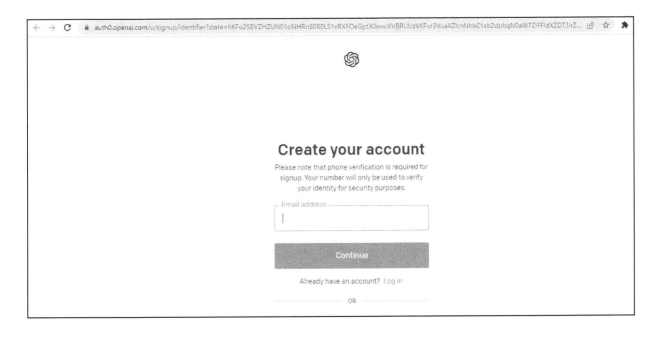

Once done, you'd have access to the free version of ChatGPT

As of April 2023, ChatGPT 3.5 is free to use and ChatGPT-4 costs $20 per month. As a beginner, you can easily test your skills on the free version.

This is how it looks:

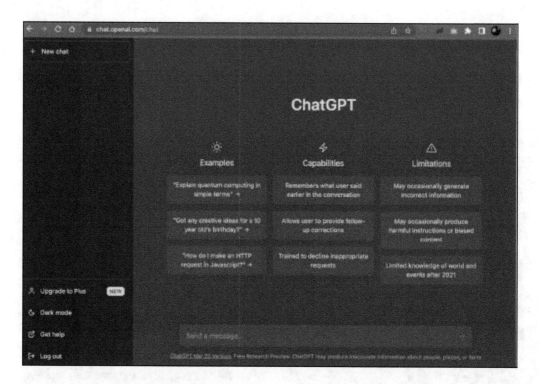

At the very bottom is where you'd chat:

You can now ask GPT anything you want, and it'll give you the desired result

Note: The procedure outlined was developed based on the instructions available at the time of writing. If you require further assistance with signing up for ChatGPT, please scan this QR code:

<u>**1.2. Bing Chat**</u>

Step 1: Go to the Microsoft website (<u>www.microsoft.com</u>).

Locate the download page for Edge or look for "Microsoft Edge" in the search bar. If you don't want to download Microsoft Edge, go directly to Step 6. For better results, we recommend using Microsoft Edge.

Step 2: Click the download button and choose the version that fits your system.

Step 3: Once downloaded, open the setup file.

Step 4: A User Account Control dialog box will appear – click "Yes" to grant permission.

The installation wizard will guide you through a series of prompts and options. Review them carefully.

Step 5: To open Microsfot Edge, press Win + R on the keyboard to open the Run window.
In the Open field, type "microsoft-edge:" and press Enter on the keyboard or click or tap OK. Microsoft Edge is now open.

Step 6: Head to bing.com/chat

Step 7: From the pop-up that appears, click 'Start chatting'

Step 8: Enter the email address for the Microsoft account you'd like to use and click 'Next'.

If you don't have one, click 'Create one!' just under the text box and follow the instructions. Enter your password when prompted and click Next. From the following screen, choose whether you'd like to stay signed in or not. Click 'Chat Now'

Step 9: Choose your conversation style. If you've never used it before, it's best to stick with 'More Balanced'

That's it! You can now start chatting.

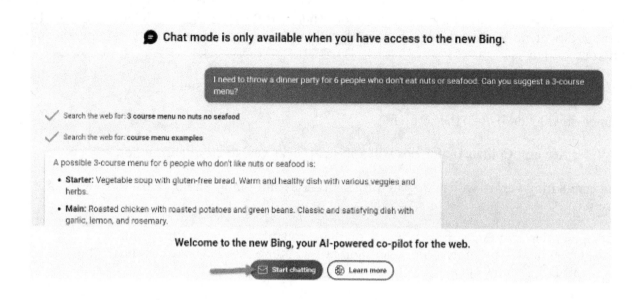

Note: The procedure outlined was developed based on the instructions available at the time of writing. If you require assistance with signing up for Bing Chat, please scan this QR code:

1.3. Google Bard

Step 1: Go to bard.google.com. Select Try Bard. Accept Google Bard Terms of Service

Step 2: Go to "Sign in"

Step 3: Enter a query or search term and then hit enter.

Wait for the AI to respond. You can then either continue the conversation or select Google It to use the traditional search engine.

Note: The procedure outlined was developed based on the instructions available at the time of writing. If you require assistance with signing up for Google Bard, please scan this QR code:

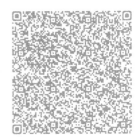

1.4. Meta LLaMA

Getting the Models

Step 1: Go to https://ai.meta.com/resources/models-and-libraries/llama-downloads/

Step 2: Fill the form with your information.

Step 3: Accept their license (if you agree with it)

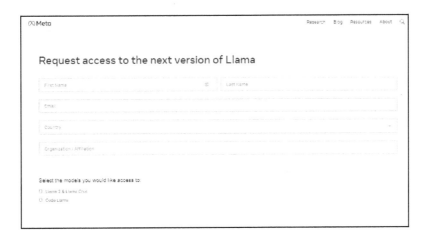

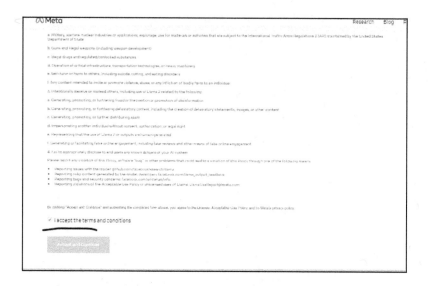

Step 4: Once your request is approved, you will receive a signed URL over email.

Step 5: Clone the Llama 2 repository (go to https://github.com/facebookresearch/llama).

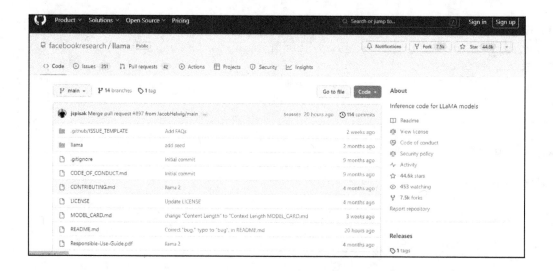

Step 6: Run the download.sh script, passing the URL provided when prompted to start the download. Keep in mind that the links expire after 24 hours and a certain amount of downloads. If you start seeing errors such as 403: Forbidden, you can always re-request a link.

Appendix No 2

Follow-up Prompts

There are 1100 prompts that you can use as follow-ups in order to get more specific or revised information from ChatGPT and other Chatbots. Don't forget to tailor these prompts to your specific circumstances and to the response you previously received from the Chatbot.

Each of these prompt types serves a different purpose and can be used effectively in different scenarios. Depending on the context and the intended outcome, one type of prompt may be more suitable than another.

These prompts are divided into eleven distinct categories, each tailored to specific conversational needs: Generic, Enhancement, Clarification, Probing, Critical Thinking, Instructional, Exploration, Comparison, Summarization, Evaluation, and Hypothetical.

To have access to 1100 follow-up prompts, please scan this QR code:

Appendix No 3

If you're new to ChatGPT, don't fret. This guide is designed to walk you through its use, step by step. By the end, you'll have a solid grasp of how to harness the power of this incredible tool.

Step 1: Accessing the Platform

Visit OpenAI's Platform: Head to OpenAI's official website: ChatGPT [openai.com]

Sign Up/Log In: If you don't have an account, you'll need to sign up. If you already have one, simply log in.

Step 2: Navigating the Interface

Dashboard: This is your central hub, where you can access various tools and see your usage stats.

Start a New Session: To interact with ChatGPT, start a new session or use a predefined platform depending on the current interface.

Step 3: Interacting with ChatGPT

Input Field: This is where you'll type or paste the prompts from our book.

Submit: Once you've entered your prompt, press 'Enter' or click the 'Submit' button.

Review Output: ChatGPT will generate a response. Take a moment to read and understand it.

Step 4: Refining Your Interaction

Being Specific: If you need specific information or a particular type of response, make your prompts more detailed.

Iterate: If the first response isn't what you're looking for, tweak your prompt and try again.

Step 5: Utilizing the Prompts from This Book

Choose a Prompt: Browse the book's prompt section and select one that aligns with your current needs.

Input: Copy and paste or type the chosen prompt into ChatGPT's input field.

Customization: Feel free to adjust the prompts to be more specific to your situation.

Step 6: Safety and Best Practices

Sensitive Information: Never share sensitive personal information, such as Social Security numbers or bank details, with ChatGPT or any online platform.

Understanding Outputs: Remember, while ChatGPT can produce human-like responses, it doesn't understand context in the same way humans do. Always review its advice with a critical eye.

Step 7: Exploring Advanced Features

As you become more comfortable with ChatGPT:

Experiment: Play around with different types of prompts to see the diverse responses you can get.

Integrate with Other Tools: There are several third-party tools and platforms that have integrated ChatGPT. Explore these to maximize your work.

Step 8: Stay Updated

Technology, especially in the AI field, evolves rapidly. Periodically check OpenAI's official channels for updates, new features, or changes to the platform.

By following this guide, even the most tech-averse individuals will find themselves comfortably navigating and interacting with ChatGPT. As we delve deeper into the book and introduce specific prompts tailored for your work you'll be equipped with the knowledge to make the most of them.

Here is our "*Elevate Your Productivity Using ChatGPT*" Guide: To access this guide to boost your efficiency and productivity, please scan this QR code.

Appendix No 4

Mentoring, Coaching, and Leadership Professionals

This list encompasses professions pivotal in nurturing growth, leadership, and collaboration in work settings. They play crucial roles in guiding, training, and inspiring individuals towards achieving personal and organizational objectives.

1. Mentor: Provides guidance, support, and wisdom to less experienced individuals for personal and professional growth.
2. Coach: Assists in developing specific skills, improving performance, and achieving defined objectives through structured guidance.
3. Leader: Guides, inspires, and influences a group towards achieving common goals, fostering positive organizational culture.
4. Executive Coach: Assists executives in honing leadership skills, achieving goals, and navigating career transitions.
5. Life Coach: Guides individuals in personal development, goal-setting, and achieving life balance.
6. Career Counselor: Provides advice on career exploration, development strategies, and job search.
7. Organizational Consultant: Aids organizations in improving performance, culture, and change management.
8. Training and Development Manager: Plans, directs, and coordinates programs to enhance employee skills.
9. Human Resources Manager: Oversees recruitment, employee relations, and organizational development.
10. Management Consultant: Advises on business strategies, problem-solving, and organizational improvements.
11. Leadership Development Specialist: Creates programs to develop leadership capabilities within organizations.
12. Performance Coach: Helps individuals improve performance and achieve professional objectives.
13. Business Coach: Guides entrepreneurs in business growth, strategy, and problem-solving.
14. Conflict Resolution Specialist: Aids in resolving disputes and improving communication in workplaces.
15. Executive Search Consultant: Assists organizations in identifying and recruiting executive leadership talent.
16. Team Building Specialist: Designs and facilitates activities to enhance team cohesion.
17. Corporate Trainer: Provides training to improve employee skills and knowledge.
18. Sales Trainer: Develops and delivers training programs to improve sales team performance and effectiveness.
19. Communication Coach: Improves interpersonal communication skills within professional settings.
20. Industrial-Organizational Psychologist: Applies psychological principles to improve workplace dynamics.
21. Change Management Consultant: Guides organizations through change with strategies to ensure smooth transitions.
22. Culture Development Consultant: Aids in cultivating a positive, productive organizational culture.
23. Educational Consultant: Advises on educational strategies, curriculum development, and leadership.
24. Talent Development Specialist: Identifies and nurtures employee talents for organizational growth.
25. Learning and Development Specialist: Designs and implements training programs to promote employee growth and organizational success.
26. Negotiation Consultant: Aids in enhancing negotiation skills and strategies.

27. Mediator: Facilitates resolution of disputes in a neutral manner.
28. Customer Service Trainer: Improves customer interaction skills of service teams.
29. Employee Engagement Consultant: Boosts employee satisfaction and productivity through engagement strategies.
30. Entrepreneurship Advisor: Guides individuals in launching and growing their own businesses.

Appendix No 5

Specializations for Mentors, Coaches and Leaders

1. This compilation presents specialized roles integral to fostering excellence, innovation, and resilience within professional landscapes, offering tailored guidance and support to propel individuals and businesses toward their aspirations.
2. Leadership: Enhancing skills for leading teams and organizations effectively.
3. Performance: Boosting individual or team productivity and output.
4. Career: Navigating career progression and transitions.
5. Sales: Increasing sales proficiency and results.
6. Marketing: Crafting and executing marketing strategies.
7. Strategy: Formulating and applying long-term business plans.
8. Innovation: Fostering creative thinking and new ideas.
9. Culture: Shaping positive organizational values and practices.
10. Conflict Resolution: Managing and resolving disputes effectively.
11. Communication Skills: Improving sharing and receiving of information.
12. Emotional Intelligence: Understanding and managing emotions for improved interactions.
13. Team Dynamics: Strengthening team cooperation and function.
14. Change Leadership: Guiding successful organizational change.
15. Diversity and Inclusion: Building respectful, diverse work environments.
16. Work-Life Balance: Balancing professional responsibilities with personal life.
17. Organizational Development: Enhancing organizational structures and efficiency.
18. Time Management: Prioritizing tasks and managing time wisely.
19. Customer Success: Ensuring clients achieve their desired outcomes.
20. Negotiation Skills: Reaching agreements effectively and advantageously.
21. Personal Branding: Crafting and communicating a personal image.
22. Corporate Governance: Directing company management and policies.
23. Business Ethics: Promoting ethical professional conduct.
24. Financial Coaching for Executives: Managing company finances and economic strategy.
25. Talent Development: Growing employee skills and career paths.
26. Digital Transformation: Integrating digital technology into all business areas.
27. Entrepreneurship: Starting and growing new business ventures.
28. Global Leadership: Leading across diverse cultures and markets.
29. Crisis Leadership: Leading effectively through emergencies.
30. Mindfulness and Well-being: Promoting mental health and mindfulness practices.

Appendix No 6

Tones

Tone reflects the emotional stance towards the subject or audience, impacting engagement and receptivity. In coaching or leadership, the right tone fosters trust, motivation, and effective communication, aligning with growth-oriented goals.

1. Motivational: Inspiring action and positivity towards achieving goals.
2. Empathetic: Demonstrating understanding and compassion towards others' experiences.
3. Authoritative: Exuding confidence and expertise in guiding others.
4. Inspirational: Provoking thought and encouraging higher aspirations.
5. Supportive: Offering encouragement and backing during challenges.
6. Reflective: Encouraging contemplation and self-assessment.
7. Directive: Providing clear, actionable guidance.
8. Analytical: Examining situations critically and logically.
9. Advisory: Offering suggestions based on expertise.
10. Challenging: Encouraging stretching beyond comfort zones.
11. Respectful: Honoring individuals' values, thoughts, and feelings.
12. Humorous: Adding levity to engage and ease tension.
13. Socratic: Encouraging critical thinking through questioning.
14. Constructive: Providing feedback for growth and improvement.
15. Patient: Showing understanding and tolerance during learning processes.
16. Optimistic: Highlighting the positive and potential success.
17. Realistic: Providing a practical and sensible perspective.
18. Encouraging: Boosting morale and self-efficacy.
19. Appreciative: Acknowledging efforts and achievements.
20. Reassuring: Alleviating concerns and instilling confidence.
21. Inquisitive: Encouraging exploration and curiosity.
22. Observational: Noting and reflecting on behaviors and outcomes.
23. Persuasive: Convincing others towards a certain viewpoint.
24. Resilient: Demonstrating toughness and adaptability in adversity.
25. Visionary: Focusing on long-term potential and broader horizons.
26. Collegial: Promoting a sense of partnership and teamwork.
27. Energizing: Infusing enthusiasm and vigor.
28. Compassionate: Showing care and understanding in dealing with others.
29. Professional: Maintaining a formal and respectful demeanor.
30. Mindful: Demonstrating awareness and consideration.

Appendix No 7

Writing Styles

Writing style denotes how ideas are expressed, encompassing word choice and narrative flow. In coaching, mentoring, and leadership, an apt style clarifies concepts, provides guidance, and facilitates meaningful exploration of ideas.

1. Expository: Explaining facts and information clearly and straightforwardly.
2. Descriptive: Painting a vivid picture to convey a particular scenario or idea.
3. Narrative: Telling a story or recounting events to convey lessons or insights.
4. Persuasive: Arguing a point or encouraging a particular action or mindset.
5. Concise: Delivering information in a brief, direct manner.
6. Analytical: Dissecting information to understand and convey underlying principles.
7. Reflective: Encouraging introspection and consideration of past experiences.
8. Dialogic: Engaging in a two-way conversation to explore ideas.
9. Illustrative: Using examples and anecdotes to clarify points.
10. Instructive: Providing detailed guidance or instructions.
11. Interpretive: Explaining and making sense of complex concepts.
12. Comparative: Analyzing similarities and differences between concepts.
13. Argumentative: Making a case for a particular stance or action.
14. Problem-Solution: Identifying issues and proposing solutions.
15. Evaluative: Assessing the value or effectiveness of certain practices.
16. Journalistic: Reporting facts in an objective, straightforward manner.
17. Exploratory: Delving into topics to discover new insights or perspectives.
18. Contemplative: Encouraging deep thought on certain topics.
19. Case Study: Delving into real-world examples to extract lessons.
20. Research-based: Grounding discourse in empirical evidence.
21. Informal: Adopting a casual, accessible approach.
22. Formal: Adhering to professional language and structure.
23. Technical: Utilizing specialized terminology relevant to the field.
24. Conceptual: Exploring ideas at a high level.
25. Practical: Focusing on actionable advice and real-world application.
26. Empirical: Relying on observation and experience.
27. Theoretical: Delving into theories and abstract concepts.
28. Storyboard: Unfolding ideas through a sequenced narrative.
29. Interactive: Encouraging active engagement from the reader.
30. Scenario-based: Outlining hypothetical situations to explore concepts.

Appendix No 8

Tags

	Chapter	Tag 1	Tag 2	Tag 3
Prompt 1	Accountability	Responsibility	Supportive Identification	Workplace Culture
Prompt 2	Accountability	Accountability	Relationships	Collaboration
Prompt 3	Accountability	Team Resilience	Problem-Solving	Supportive Leadership
Prompt 4	Accountability	Task Prioritization	Team Autonomy	Efficiency Enhancement
Prompt 5	Accountability	Goal Achievement	Ambition Cultivation	Success Strategies
Prompt 6	Awareness	Resource Optimization	Allocation Efficiency	Task Management
Prompt 7	Awareness	Positive Mindset	Motivation Maintenance	Supportive Leadership
Prompt 8	Awareness	Ideal Self	Self-Awareness	Professional Growth
Prompt 9	Awareness	Questioning	Insight	Understanding
Prompt 10	Awareness	Mindset	Positive	Conversion
Prompt 11	Awareness	Barriers	Detection	Progress
Prompt 12	Belief	Hindrance	Development	Mindset
Prompt 13	Belief	Assessment	Engagement	Strategies
Prompt 14	Belief	Core-Values	Behavior	Professionalism
Prompt 15	Belief	Awareness	Outcomes	Decision-Making
Prompt 16	Belief	Motivation	Analysis	Evidence
Prompt 17	Challenge	Innovation	Encouragement	Challenges
Prompt 18	Challenge	Self-awareness	Decision-Making	Beliefs
Prompt 19	Challenge	Data	Relevance	Strategies
Prompt 20	Challenge	Problem-Solving	Cultivation	Empowerment
Prompt 21	Challenge	Team-Motivation	Leadership	Empowerment
Prompt 22	Challenge	Comfort-Zone	Performance	Team-Dynamics
Prompt 23	Change	Change-Management	Innovation	Adaptability
Prompt 24	Change	Forward-Thinking	Impact	Strategy
Prompt 25	Change	Prioritization	Decision-Making	Task-Management
Prompt 26	Commitment	Influence	Commitment	Goal-Orientation
Prompt 27	Commitment	Composure	Support	Well-being
Prompt 28	Creativity	Creativity	Problem-Solving	Innovation
Prompt 29	Creativity	Creativity	Enhancement	Responsibilities
Prompt 30	Decisions	Meetings	Communication	Management
Prompt 31	Decisions	Engagement	Discussion	Empowerment
Prompt 32	Excitement	Persuasion	Investors	Excitement
Prompt 33	Excitement	Energy	Enhancement	Transition
Prompt 34	Excitement	Feedback	Recognition	Empowerment
Prompt 35	Fear	Empowerment	Ambition	Anxiety
Prompt 36	Feelings	Empathy	Relationships	Improvement
Prompt 37	Feelings	Mental-Health	Support	Management
Prompt 38	Feelings	Conversations	Understanding	Significance
Prompt 39	Flow	Motivation	Productivity	Energy
Prompt 40	Flow	Empowerment	Focus	Productivity
Prompt 41	Fulfillment	Guidance	Objectives	Potential
Prompt 42	Goals	Purpose	Professional	Personal

Prompt 43	Goals	Synergy	Goal	Frameworks
Prompt 44	Goals	Monitoring	Intervention	Accountability
Prompt 45	Goals	Professionalism	Improvement	Objectives
Prompt 46	Habits	Competency	Assessment	Talent-Assessment
Prompt 47	Habits	Patterns	Management	Team-Development
Prompt 48	Learning	Learning	Techniques	Comprehension
Prompt 49	Learning	Experiences	Beliefs	Self-Awareness
Prompt 50	Learning	Blindspots	Leadership	Biases
Prompt 51	Learning	Identification	Application	Performance
Prompt 52	Learning	PositiveCulture	Productivity	KnowledgeTransfer
Prompt 53	Learning	ContinuousLearning	Self-awareness	LessonLearned
Prompt 54	Learning	Authenticity	Communication	Introspection
Prompt 55	Learning	Leadership	Risk-Management	Reflection
Prompt 56	Listening	Problem-Solving	Bottleneck-Identification	Innovation
Prompt 57	Mindset	Work-Environment	Empowerment	Assessment
Prompt 58	Mindset	Team-Dynamics	Awareness	Questioning
Prompt 59	Mindset	Possibilities	Reflection	Engagement
Prompt 60	Mindset	Empathy	Career	Feedback
Prompt 61	Mindset	Readiness	Team-Dynamics	Project-Management
Prompt 62	Options	Opportunities	Development	Learning
Prompt 63	Options	Stability	Individual-Preferences	Human-Resources
Prompt 64	Options	Decision-Making	Transparency	Leadership
Prompt 65	Performance	Self-Awareness	Performance	Coaching
Prompt 66	Performance	Communication	Trust-Building	Inclusivity
Prompt 67	Performance	Achievement	Self-Reflection	Marketing
Prompt 68	Preferences	Trust-building	Mentorship	OpenDialogue
Prompt 69	Priorities	Goal-setting	Finance	Strategic Planning
Prompt 70	Progress	Well-being	Mental-Health	Productivity
Prompt 71	Progress	Planning	Project-Management	Collaboration
Prompt 72	Progress	Motivation	OrganizationalBehavior	Stagnation
Prompt 73	Purpose	Emotional	Articulation	Morale
Prompt 74	Purpose	Commitment	Dialogue	Performance
Prompt 75	Purpose	Engagement	Purpose	Satisfaction
Prompt 76	Relationships	Resilience	Problem-Solving	Support
Prompt 77	Relationships	Perception	Alignment	Duties
Prompt 78	Relationships	Empowerment	Leadership	Self-awareness
Prompt 79	Relationships	Assessment	Leadership	Analytical
Prompt 80	Relationships	Collaboration	Accountability	Consultative
Prompt 81	Relationships	Recognition	Interpersonal	Reflective
Prompt 82	Relationships	Leadership	Effectiveness	Performance
Prompt 83	Relationships	Self-assessment	Motivation	Development
Prompt 84	Relationships	Engagement	Tools	Creativity
Prompt 85	Relationships	Reflective	Resourcefulness	Collaboration
Prompt 86	Self-assessment	Leadership	Persuasion	Executive
Prompt 87	Self-assessment	Engagement	Passions	Cohesion
Prompt 88	Self-assessment	Communication	Observational	Strategies
Prompt 89	Skills	Benchmarking	Development	Prioritization
Prompt 90	Skills	Prioritization	Effectiveness	Diagnostics

Prompt 91	Strategies	Impediments	Proactive	Mitigation
Prompt 92	Strength	Exhilaration	Strengths	Challenges
Prompt 93	Strength	Strengths	Engagement	Team-Dynamics
Prompt 94	Strength	Ownership	Self-awareness	Strengths
Prompt 95	Strength	Exploration	Assets	Forward-thinking
Prompt 96	Strength	Overextension	Self-awareness	Diagnostics
Prompt 97	Strength	Transparency	Authenticity	Investigation
Prompt 98	Strength	Misalignment	Assessment	Realignment
Prompt 99	Support	Assumptions	Decision-Making	Risk Management
Prompt 100	Support	Patience	Empathy	Reflective
Prompt 101	Support	System Analysis	KPIs	Scalability
Prompt 102	Support	Resilience	Communication	Emotional Intelligence
Prompt 103	Values	Self-reflection	Values	Identity
Prompt 104	Values	Alignment	CoreValues	Tangible
Prompt 105	Values	Roadmap	Alignment	TeamValues
Prompt 106	Values	Dialogue	Leadership	Values
Prompt 107	Weakness	Evaluation	Abilities	Talent
Prompt 108	Weakness	Articulation	EmotionalIQ	SelfAwareness
Prompt 109	Weakness	Overlooked	Management	Opportunities
Prompt 110	Weakness	Self-Improvement	Experience	Reflective
Prompt 111	Weakness	Performance	Qualities	Empowerment

Appendix No 9

Unlock the Full Potential of This Book - Instantly

Dive into a world of convenience with our electronic copy! Feel free to seamlessly copy and paste any prompt that sparks your interest.

Customize them to fit your unique needs. Say goodbye to the hassle of retyping. Start crafting your perfect prompts with ease and efficiency!.

To access the electronic copy, please scan this QR code:

www.ingramcontent.com/pod-product-compliance
Lightning Source LLC
LaVergne TN
LVHW082036050326

832904LV00005B/202

* 9 7 8 1 9 9 8 4 0 2 1 7 5 *